101
Complaint
Letters
That Get
Results

101
Complaint Letters
That Get
Results

Janet Rubel
Attorney at Law

SPHINX® PUBLISHING
AN IMPRINT OF SOURCEBOOKS, INC.®
NAPERVILLE, ILLINOIS
www.SphinxLegal.com

First Edition, 2003
Second Printing: April, 2004

Published by: **Sphinx® Publishing, An Imprint of Sourcebooks, Inc.®**

<u>Naperville Office</u>
P.O. Box 4410
Naperville, Illinois 60567-4410
630-961-3900
Fax: 630-961-2168
www.sourcebooks.com
www.SphinxLegal.com

This publication is designed to provide accurate and authoritative information in regard to the subject matter covered. It is sold with the understanding that the publisher is not engaged in rendering legal, accounting, or other professional service. If legal advice or other expert assistance is required, the services of a competent professional person should be sought.

From a Declaration of Principles Jointly Adopted by a Committee of the American Bar Association and a Committee of Publishers and Associations

This product is not a substitute for legal advice.

Disclaimer required by Texas statutes.

Library of Congress Cataloging-in-Publication Data
Rubel, Janet.
   101 complaint letters that get results : an attorney writes the choice
words that say what you mean and get the satisfaction you deserve! / by
Janet Rubel.
      p. cm.
   Accompanying CD-ROM contains letter templates.
   ISBN 1-57248-363-6 (alk. paper)
   1. Complaint letters. 2. Consumer complaints. I. Title: One hundred
one complaint letters that get results. II. Title: One hundred and one
complaint letters that get results. III. Title: Complaint letters that
get results. IV. Title.

HF5415.52 .R83 2003
381.3--dc22
                                        2003021549

Printed and bound in the United States of America.

VHG 10 9 8 7 6 5 4 3 2

Dedication

This book is dedicated to my family: my late mother, Betty, who would be "kvelling," with pride if she could read this (and passing copies out to her friends and total strangers); my husband and personal computer consultant, Alan; and my beautiful, witty daughters Amanda and Rebecca.

Acknowledgment

I am grateful to Dianne Wheeler, the division manager of Sphinx Publishing. She is informed, pleasant, and helpful. Kelly Barrales-Saylor is the skilled production editor whose suggestions made this a better book.

The support of my friends and family inspired me: my favorite Pi Phi Elizabeth Naylor; friends Teri Heyden, Carol Freibaum and Barb Leff; my brother Howard Strong, the first lawyer/author in our family; my brother Craig Strange, another published author; and my brother Gerald Strange, a lawyer/writer. The wise ladies in Esther's water aerobics class shared their consumer problems with me and offered encouragement.

My alma mater, Washington University, provided a wonderful education and lifelong friendships.

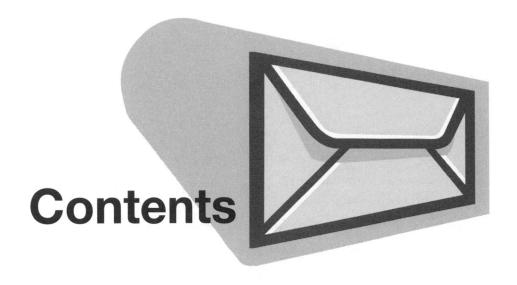

Contents

Introduction . . . . **xvii**

Chapter 1: CARS **1**

Lemon Laws

Odometer Fraud

Consumer Protection

Insurance

Financing

Credit Life Insurance

Taking Action—Step-by-Step

 Letter 1: Lemon Laws

 Letter 2: Lemon Laws; Second Letter to Dealership

 Letter 3: Odometer Fraud on Used Car

 Letter 4: Odometer Fraud; Second Letter to Dealership

 Letter 5: Odometer Fraud; Follow-Up to Manufacturer

 Letter 6: Insurance Claim; Repairs Made with Used Parts

 Letter 7: Insurance Claim; Follow-Up for Non-Payment

 Letter 8: Credit Life Insurance Assessed on Car Loan

Chapter 2: COMPUTERS **17**

    Defective Computer Merchandise

    Internet Service

    Internet Crimes

    Online Purchases

    Spam (Unwanted Commercial Email)

    Taking Action—Step-by-Step

        Letter 9: Defective Computer

        Letter 10: Defective Merchandise; Computer Incompatibility

        Letter 11: Defective Merchandise; Incompatible Software

        Letter 12: Internet Service; Lack of Security

        Letter 13: Internet Crime; Stolen Information

        Letter 14: Online Purchase; Shipment not Received

        Letter 15: Online Purchase not Received; Second Letter to Company

        Letter 16: Spam

        Letter 17: Spam; Violating State Law

Chapter 3: EMPLOYMENT **35**

    Discrimination

    Equal Pay

    Mental or Physical Disabilities

    Age Discrimination

    Sexual Harassment

    Family and Medical Leave Act

    Employee Records

    Taking Action—Step-by-Step

        Letter 18: Race Discrimination; Letter to Human Resources Department

        Letter 19: Religious Discrimination; Letter to Direct Supervisor

        Letter 20: Unequal Pay

        Letter 21: Handicapped Accommodation

        Letter 22: Failure to Accommodate Disability; Follow-Up to Manager

        Letter 23: Age Discrimination

        Letter 24: Sexual Harassment; Follow-Up to Human Resources Manager

        Letter 25: Paternity Leave Request; Follow-Up to Human Resources Department

        Letter 26: Unpaid Family Leave of Absence

        Letter 27: Review Employment Records

        Letter 28: Employee's Statement to be Added to Employment Record

Chapter 4: FINANCES 53

Credit Cards

Debit Cards

Collecting a Debt

Credit Reports

Insurance Bills

Investments

Members of the Military

Taking Action—Step-by-Step

Letter 29: Credit Card Company; Received Damaged Product

Letter 30: Credit Card Company; Second Letter, Dispute Charge

Letter 31: Credit Card Company; Error on Statement

Letter 32: Credit Card Company; Late Charge Assessed

Letter 33: Credit Card Company; Unauthorized Use after a Divorce

Letter 34: Bank; Unauthorized Transaction on Debit Card

Letter 35: Bank; Debit Card Used to Empty Checking Account

Letter 36: Dispute with Bank; Unauthorized Use of Debit Card

Letter 37: Dispute with Collection Agency; Alleged Debt

Letter 38: Collection Agency; Second Letter, Disputing Alleged Debt

Letter 39: Credit Agency; Negative Credit Report

Letter 40: Credit Agency; Errors in Credit Report

Letter 41: Insurance Billing Error

Letter 42: Hospital; Second Letter, Insurance Billing Error

Letter 43: Liquidation of Brokerage Account

Letter 44: Follow-Up Letter to Securities Exchange, Liquidation of Brokerage Account

Letter 45: Securities Exchange Commission; Reporting Brokerage Violations

Letter 46: Credit Card Company; Reduction in Interest Rate due to Military Service

Chapter 5: HEALTH 83

Health Insurance Portability and Accountability Act (HIPAA)

Billing Errors

Prescription Drug Coverage Refusal

Denial of Coverage

Uninsured Patient

Hospital Accreditation

Nursing Homes

Health Care Power of Attorney and Living Wills

Pharmacy/Prescription Complaints

Fair Debt Collection Practices Act

Taking Action—Step-by-Step

    Letter 47: Doctor's Employees Violated Privacy Act

    Letter 48: Doctor's Office; Second Letter, Concerning Violation of Privacy

    Letter 49: Department of Health; Follow-Up Letter, Violation of Privacy

    Letter 50: Health Insurance; Billing Error

    Letter 51: Health Insurance; Refusal of Prescription Drug

    Letter 52: Health Insurance; Second Letter, Reconsider Refusal of Prescription Drug

    Letter 53: Health Insurance; Claims Clerk Error

    Letter 54: Health Insurance; Denial of Coverage

    Letter 55: Hospital; Uninsured Patient

    Letter 56: Hospital; Unclean Facilities and Poor Care

    Letter 57: Nursing Home; Lack of Acceptable Care

    Letter 58: Hospital; Life Support for Relative

    Letter 59: Hospital; Power of Attorney for Healthcare

    Letter 60: Mail Order Pharmacy; Dispute Charges and Service

    Letter 61: Collection Agency; Cease Contact

Chapter 6: HOME **109**

Safety Conditions

Home Improvement

Housing Discrimination

Security Deposits

Private Mortgage Insurance (PMI)

Do Not Call Registry

Spam

Delay in Shipment

Soldier's and Sailor's Relief Act of 1940

    Letter 62: Tenant Injured on Rental Property

    Letter 63: Carpet Company; Contract Terms not Honored

    Letter 64: Cable Company; Missed Appointment

    Letter 65: Utility Company; Failure to Mark Utilities

    Letter 66: Real Estate Company; Discriminatory Practice—Race

Letter 67: Rental Company; Refusal to Rent—Children

Letter 68: Property Management Company; Return of Security Deposit

Letter 69: Bank; Cancel Private Mortgage Insurance (PMI)

Letter 70: Bank; Cancel Private Mortgage Insurance (PMI)

Letter 71: Bank; Second Letter to Cancel Private Mortgage Insurance (PMI)

Letter 72: Company; Remove Customer from Call List

Letter 73: State Do Not Call Registry; Report Violation

Letter 74: Federal Do Not Call registry; Report Violation

Letter 75: Internet Service Provider; Spam Problem

Letter 76: Internet Provider; Second Letter, Cancel Service

Letter 77: Internet Adviser; Delete Name from Email List

Letter 78: Federal Trade Commission (FTC); Internet Advertiser Refusal to Remove Name from List

Letter 79: Catalog Order not Received

Letter 80: Catalog Company; Second Letter, Order Information

Letter 81: Catalog Company; Third Letter, FTC Violation

Letter 82: Mortgage Company; Second Letter, Reduce Mortgage Interest Rate for Military

Chapter 7: SCHOOL 141

Individual with Educational Disabilities Act

Bullying

Taking Action—Step-by-Step

Letter 83: Principal; Follow-Up Letter, Screening Child for Learning Disability

Letter 84: Principal; Second Letter, Need to Develop Education Plan

Letter 85: Principal; Third Letter, Child's Right to Individualized Educational Evaluation (IEE)

Letter 86: Principal; Bullying of Child

Letter 87: Principal; Second Letter, Bullying of Child

Letter 88: Superintendent of Schools; Follow-Up Letter, Bullying of Child

Chapter 8: TRAVEL. **155**

Damaged or Lost Luggage

Passengers with Disabilities

Travel Agents

Bumped Airline Passengers

Hotels and Other Public Places

Trains

Taxicabs

Car Rental

Letter 89: Airline; Lost Luggage

Letter 90: Department of Transportation; Repair Luggage

Letter 91: Department of Transportation; Stolen Item

Letter 92: Department of Transportation; Failure to Accommodate Passenger with Disability

Letter 93: Department of Transportation; Screening Discrimination

Letter 94: Trade Organization; Travel Agency Theft

Letter 95: Airlines; Bumped Passenger

Letter 96: Hotel; Quoted Reservation

Letter 97: Hotel; Handicapped Access

Letter 98: Hotel; Misrepresentation of Facility

Letter 99: Railroad; Unsatisfactory Accommodations

Letter 100: Department of Consumer Services; Inflated Taxi Charges

Letter 101: Car Rental Company; Breach of Contract

Appendix A: STATE ATTORNEYS GENERAL **181**

Appendix B: STATE SECURITIES ADMINISTRATORS **191**

Appendix C: STATE DEPARTMENT OF
                INSURANCE REGULATORS **207**

Appendix D: STATE DO NOT CALL INFORMATION. **219**

**Appendix E: U.S. MILITARY CONSUMER
          SERVICES PROGRAMS**. 227

**Appendix F: AUTOMOBILE MANUFACTURERS'
          CUSTOMER SERVICE DEPARTMENTS**. 231

Index. 243

About the Author 247

Introduction

Misfortune can strike at any point in your life. Whether it is a recurring problem with a car or a billing problem with a credit card company, there are numerous things that can go wrong. Sometimes it is difficult to resolve even the simplest matters because anger or frustration gets in the way. The letters and information in this book will help you find a solution by taking the emotion out of the complaint.

The first step you should take to resolve any complaint is to gather all the facts and related papers. Read all warranties and guarantees, if you have them.

If you have a complaint about a particular store, call the store and ask to speak to the manager or customer service department. Always be polite. If that does not work, send a letter. Be brief and include only the relevant facts. Send copies of the necessary papers.

If you have a complaint about healthcare, contact the hospital ombudsman or your doctor's office. For a billing problem, ask the billing department to review the bill. Always get an itemized bill. For a quality complaint, contact the ombudsman at the hospital or the head nurse of the unit. If that does not resolve the problem, then contact the president of the hospital or the head of the doctor's department.

The Better Business Bureau is a nonprofit group that works to prevent dishonest business practices. It conducts a complaint resolution service for various problems including automobile dealer issues. Look in your local telephone book or search the internet for your local chapter.

A trade group may have a resolution process to handle problems such as travel agent complaints. Research the various trade groups and learn which business, if any, the agent causing you problems belongs.

As a last resort, you may take your problem to Small Claims Court. Most states and localities have simple, consumer-friendly court systems. An attorney may not be needed. Judges sitting in these courts are usually very skilled in resolving complaints. Most court systems have the necessary forms on the Internet. You can also pick up the necessary forms in person at the courthouse.

NOTE: *The clerks cannot give you legal advice, but they may be able to assist you in filling out the forms.*

Author's Note: This book is intended to be a guide for consumers, but not intended to be legal advice. You should consult your own legal advisor to obtain information pertinent to your situation. If you cannot afford an attorney, you may qualify for legal aid. Call your local bar association for details. For those who cannot qualify for legal aid, there may be help available at law school clinics or charitable legal assistance clinics. Ask your local reference librarian for resource information. Look on the Internet for lawyers who handle certain problems without a payment.

How to Use this Book

This book is unique in that it contains information you can use to understand your rights as a consumer, samples of letters, and a CD with customizable letters that you can complete and print from your computer.

Each chapter is divided into two sections—the consumer reference sumary and the sample letters. Each letter is completed for a specific incident to demonstrate the appropriate wording for a particular type of complaint.

For every sample letter, there is a corresponding blank letter on the CD. Start by reading the chapter material to learn more about your rights in regards to the situation you are in. Find a letter that generally matches your situation and study its wording. When you are ready, open the corresponding letter on the CD. The skeleton of the letter is already there, but there are blank portions for you to complete with your own details. Refer back to the sample letter for examples of appropriate entries.

When you have completed your letter, print it out and sign your name in ink just above your printed name at the bottom of the page. Use the appendices in the back of the book to find agencies and organizations to assist you in getting results with your complaint.

1 Cars

For most people, the purchase or lease of a car is one of the most expensive items they will ever buy. A car is necessary for many of us to commute to work, to take our children to school and to their many activities, and for our convenience.

Car dealers are a source of many consumer complaints—from bogus processing fees added to the sales contract, to defective repairs and unreliable new cars. Consult the federal, state, and local laws to determine the permitted fees and charges. Dealers may try to increase their profit by adding fees such as, *loan processing, warehousing fee, advertising fee, paperwork fee, administrative costs,* or other pure profit items. You do not have to pay any of these fees. Read your financial documents very carefully.

Lemon Laws

State and federal laws exist to protect consumers from defective new cars, shoddy repairs, and used car sales. The state and federal laws that protect the consumer from defective new cars are called *lemon laws.*

Each state has its own laws and rules that must be followed in order to preserve your rights. For example, some states require the dealer to make *three* attempts to fix the car before you can demand a new car. Other states require *four* visits before the dealer must replace the *lemon.*

There are state and federal laws that require automobile dealers and manufacturers to repair and/or replace defective new cars. If you have the misfortune of buying one of these, learn your rights under your state laws. The state where you purchased the car is the applicable law to follow. Your state attorney general has helpful information about the law and your rights as a car purchaser and owner. Large cities often have their own consumer departments and laws concerning cars. An excellent website with links to each state's law is **www.lemonlawssa.com**.

Many states require the dealer to give you a new car *or* to refund your purchase price if you have purchased a lemon. When taking in your car for repairs, always get a written work order that specifies that you are having *warranty work* performed. An unscrupulous dealer may argue that you brought the car in for another reason and therefore he or she is not liable for replacing your car. Many states require that the defects prevent you from using the car for thirty days or more in total or that the dealer has made four attempts to fix the vehicle. The only way you will prove your case is to have good records.

You must keep careful records of the dates of the problems and repair attempts. Each time the car is taken to the mechanic, record the reason for the visit and the date of the visit. Keep all paperwork and be sure to read the paperwork, warranties, and guarantees. Try to avoid paying cash. Charge repairs on your credit card so you have some recourse if the repairs are not made properly. You can ask the credit card company to refuse to pay the repair shop until you are satisfied with the job.

Odometer Fraud

The United States Department of Transportation National Highway Traffic Safety Administration estimates that more than half of all vehicles sold by leasing companies have *odometer tampering*. Leasing companies often turn back the odometer on a high-mileage, late model car to defraud the consumer into believing that the vehicle has much lower mileage. The consumer then purchases a vehicle that is not worth the purchase price. The titles to these cars are often transferred from state to state in order to make the history of the car harder to trace for the buyer.

Most often, a car with high mileage has more repair problems. The unwary buyer will spend more for repairs than he or she would expect. This can add thousands of dollars to the purchase price and the car might not even run at all, making it almost worthless. The dealer commits fraud when he or she misrepresents the value and nature of the car. It is important for a buyer to do his or her homework before purchasing a vehicle.

Never buy a used car without first having your mechanic inspect the car on his or her premises. The *VIN (vehicle identification number)* should be traced through an Internet service. The dealer should reveal whether the car has been in an accident, flood or fire, and whether it has been rebuilt—ask these specific questions. A search of the VIN number will reveal the car's history for any accidents, plus its accurate mileage.

Be alert if you see that the title is from out-of-state. Have your mechanic check your car. Is the wear and tear consistent with the miles reported by the seller? Check the truth of the odometer reading for free at the Carfax website at **www.odometeraccuracycheck.com**. You will need to have the seventeen character vehicle identification number (VIN) in order to run this odometer check. The VIN is located on the dashboard.

If the mileage is much higher than represented to you, then you have the proof you need to return the car for the purchase price. Contact the dealer as soon as you know that the odometer was reset. You have the common law right to *rescind* a contract entered into because of the fraud by the dealer. A *rescission* of the sale means that you are canceling the entire sale with the dealer. You are erasing the transaction, as if it had never occurred.

Rescission is a remedy for fraud in the inducement of a contract. In other words, the dealer's representation that the car had fewer miles induced you to purchase the car. You would not have paid the same price for a car with 150,000 miles, as a car with 50,000 miles.

Contact the dealer and try to resolve the problem. Document your visit and send your letters by certified mail. Take another person with you if you visit the dealer, such as a friend. You will have another witness to verify your account of the odometer trouble. Should the dealer be unwilling to refund your money, then you should contact the dealer's corporate offices. Start by contacting the zone customer service office. Next, contact the corporate headquarter's customer service department. If this is not helpful, then contact the legal office or the general counsel's office. (Lawyers take fraud very seriously.)

If you purchased your car with a false odometer reading at a dealer affiliated with a well-known brand such as Ford, Chrysler, General Motors, Saab, Toyota, Subaru, Mitsubishi, or others, then you have more alternatives for relief. Automobile manufacturers do not want bad publicity, especially of this type. It can and should require the errant dealer to refund your money. The manufacturer is liable for the acts of the dealer because the dealer is the agent of the manufacturer.

In addition, odometer tampering constitutes civil fraud and criminal fraud in most states. You can sue for your money back and damages in civil court *and* possibly send the perpetrator to jail. Be careful in trying to collect your money. You cannot threaten someone with jail in order to collect a debt. File a criminal complaint with your local prosecutor if you have problems collecting your debt.

Consumer Protection

Consumer protection agencies have pamphlets for potential buyers that contain helpful advice to avoid dealer fraud. Buyers who finance the purchase or lease of their vehicles should read consumer finance advice from one of these agencies, too. For example, a common car dealer scam is to have the consumer sign a blank finance contract, promising to fill in the agreed upon terms later. The dealer then inserts higher rates and a higher price unknown to the buyer. *Never sign a blank contract.*

There are consumer protection lawyers who will review your case if you have been overcharged or defrauded by a car dealer. Call your local bar association for referrals. The lawyer may not charge a fee if he or she takes your case, as some types of cases require the car dealer or finance company to pay your legal fees and costs.

State consumer watchdog organizations, such as the state attorney general, may sue the dealer on your behalf. There may be a *class action suit* for particularly outrageous dealer behavior. (This is a lawsuit in which one person sues on behalf of all others who have the same problem.)

The *Better Business Bureau* operates an arbitration service for car dealer complaints. Check your local chapter for details. This is a voluntary out-of-court forum for resolving your complaint. A third party, the arbitrator, hears from the car dealer and you, the owner. A decision is given and it is enforceable if the consumer accepts the decision. The car dealer must obey the ruling.

Insurance

What happens if your insurance company refuses to pay your claim after an accident? Do you have any recourse? This chapter cannot cover all aspects of vehicles and insurance, but there is enough guidance here to enable you to be a more informed consumer.

Each state regulates the sale of insurance. The state authorities can revoke the license of an insurance company or agent that does not pay legitimate claims. There are *substandard insurance companies* that make a practice of routinely rejecting claims for automobile accidents. They hope that if they reject your legitimate claim often enough, you will give up. Do not let them get away with this! Complain to the state authorities.

Insurance companies that specialize in selling insurance to drivers with poor records are called *substandard*. These companies generate many complaints from consumers for failure to pay claims. Your own insurance company may help you to collect the claim through the process of *subrogation*. Your vehicle will be repaired by your company even though the other driver is at fault, in return for you agreeing to assign your right to collect damages from the other driver's insurance company. Then, the other driver's company will be liable for the cost. Ask your insurance agent for information. Always report an accident to your own insurance company, immediately.

Until a recent class action lawsuit, insurance companies repaired cars with other than new parts. Consumers sued and successfully argued that the insurance companies should be using new parts to repair their vehicles. As a result, you have the right to insist that only new, manufacturer replacement parts are used in your car, not generic or rebuilt parts. The purpose of insurance is to restore your vehicle to its pre-crash condition. If the insurance company balks at using manufacturer recommended parts in the repairs, then tell the company you would prefer a new car.

Financing

Federal and state laws regulate the extension of consumer credit. The terms of the loan, including annual percentage rate (APR), monthly payment, and term of the loan, must be disclosed on the face of the loan documents. If you believe that you have been preyed upon, consult your state attorney general or the agency responsible for enforcing consumer laws in your state.

Also consider consulting a consumer lawyer. These lawyers may not charge for a consultation. Consumer lawyers may not charge you an individual fee because the creditor must pay their fees if the case is successful. Also, you may be part of a class action suit where the creditor, not you, pays the fees.

The Better Business Bureau (BBB) in your area may offer mediation and arbitration of car sales disputes. Their website for this kind of problem can be found at: **www.dr.bbb.org/autoline**.

Credit Life Insurance

Credit Life Insurance is sold to buyers who purchase items on credit such as cars, appliances, and electronics. The insurer promises to make your payments if you are ill and cannot work. These policies rarely make the promised payments because the policy fine print has so many conditions and exclusions. Credit Life Insurance is highly profitable for the seller. It is rarely a good buy for the consumer. The premiums are added into the finance price of the sale, thus increasing the amount of money you owe.

Taking Action—Step-By-Step

1. Contact seller of vehicle.

2. If you do not receive satisfaction from the seller, contact the regional office of the automobile manufacturer, called the *zone office*. Ask the regional manager to resolve your problem. If this does not solve your problem, go to the corporate headquarters for help. If you have a warranty, check to see if the warranty covers the problem.

3. If you purchased your vehicle from somewhere other than an automobile dealer, send a certified letter to the seller outlining the problem and describing the action you want the seller to take to fix your problem.

4. After about ten business days, if you still have not received any response to your certified letter, contact your local government consumer affairs office, if you live in a large metropolitan area. If you purchased the car from a dealer, contact your state attorney general or the Better Business Bureau.

5. Remember that odometer fraud or selling a wrecked car as new is a crime. You may want to contact the police.

6. Finally, contact an attorney. Lawyers specializing in *lemon laws* are available in every state. Call your local bar association. Look on the Internet under *lemon law attorneys*. You may also sue the person or company that sold you the vehicle in small claims court by yourself, if you cannot get a lawyer to take your case.

Letter 1: Lemon Laws

Easy Rider
9851 Redstone Circle
Fort Wayne, Indiana 29434
555-555-0000

November 12, 2003

Hoosier Friendly Car Dealership
Ms. Linda Larson
General Manager
2764 Highway 100
Fort Wayne, Indiana 29434

Re: Defective New Car

Dear Ms. Larson:

Please be advised that I purchased a new 2003 automobile, a Capitol Cruiser, from your dealership on November 1, 2003. The car broke down on the way home from your dealership—the day I bought it.

You towed it back to the dealership and promised me it would be repaired by November 15. I picked it up from your showroom over the weekend. The electrical system gave out again on my way home.

You now have the car in your garage for repairs of the same problem for the third time in less than one month. If it is not repaired to my satisfaction this time, I shall rescind the sale. A copy of the sales contract is enclosed.

Very truly yours,

Easy Rider
Cc:enc:file

Letter 2: Lemon Laws; Second Letter to Dealership

Easy Rider
9851 Redstone Circle
Fort Wayne, Indiana 29434
555-555-0000

November 22, 2003

Hoosier Friendly Car Dealership
Ms. Linda Larson
General Manager
2764 Highway 100
Fort Wayne, Indiana 29434

Re: Defective New Car

Dear Ms. Larson:

I am writing to inform you that the new car I purchased from you on November 1, still does not work, despite your best efforts to repair the car. Once again, the electrical system failed and the car died as soon as I drove more than a few feet. The car was towed to your dealership.

This is the last chance I am giving you to fix the car. If the car does not function as a new car should—flawlessly—then I shall expect to have this car replaced with a brand new Cruiser. I also request reimbursement for the cost of a rental care I had to use because my new car does not work. A copy of the bill for the rental is enclosed.

Very truly yours,

Easy Rider
Cc:enc:file
Cc:Capitol Car Company Customer Service

Letter 3: Odometer Fraud on Used Car

Gullible Buyer
220 Arlington Road
Very Cold, MN 30167
333-255-5555

May 20, 2003

Owner
Viking Motors
800 Norse Blvd.
Very Cold, MN 30167

Re: Odometer Fraud

Dear Mr. Conniver:

I am writing concerning the used car I purchased from your dealership on June 8. Your salesman told me the car was lightly used, having only 24,800 miles on it. The odometer reading was 24,800. Once I drove the car home, it had many problems.

I took the car to my mechanic. He advised me that the car had a lot of miles and had been fixed after an accident. I checked the VIN history and learned that the car has closer to 80,000 miles on it. The car had been in an accident and rebuilt—a fact that was not disclosed to me.

Therefore, I am rescinding the purchase of this car. Your salesperson misrepresented a material fact that I relied on in deciding to purchase the car.

Please call me to discuss the arrangements for the return of the car and for the refund of my purchase price of $18,000.00.

Very truly yours,

Gullible Buyer
Cc:file

Letter 4: Odometer Fraud; Second Letter to Dealership

Gullible Buyer
220 Arlington Road
Very Cold, MN 30167
333-255-5555

May 27, 2003

Owner
Viking Motors
800 Norse Blvd.
Very Cold, MN 30167

Re: Odometer Fraud

Dear Mr. Conniver:

I have not heard from you concerning the rescission of the purchase of my car.

The car will be returned to you on June 1, 2003 at 9 A.M. Unless I receive a cashier's check for the full amount of my purchase price of $18,000.00, I shall take legal action, immediately.

Very truly yours,

Gullible Buyer
Cc:file

Letter 5: Odometer Fraud; Follow-Up to Manufacturer

Gullible Buyer
220 Arlington Road
Very Cold, MN 30167
333-255-5555

June 1, 2003

Customer Service Department
Spectacular Automobile Manufacturing Co.
99 Roadster Blvd.
Detroit, MI 44098

Re: Viking Motors Odometer Fraud

Dear Sir or Madam:

Please be advised that I purchased a car from your dealer, Viking Motors. I found after the purchase that the odometer had been turned back from about 80,000 miles to 24,000 miles. Enclosed are copies of my correspondence with the dealership trying to return the car and to receive a refund of my purchase price. The dealer has not responded. The manager at the dealership refused to accept the car when I tried to return it this morning.

Unless I receive a refund of my purchase price of $18,000 within seven days, I shall have no choice but to pursue my legal remedies. I am prepared to return the car at anytime you direct. It is currently in my garage.

Very truly yours,

Gullible Buyer
Cc:enc:file

Letter 6: Insurance Claim; Repairs Made with Used Parts

Michael Motorist
88 Seashell Dr.
Savannah, GA 05347
555-555-1255

October 2, 2003

Pilgrim Insurance Co.
33 Beacon St.
Boston, MA 23767

Re: Policy #L-550896

Dear Sir or Madam:

On May 15, 2003, my car was hit by another automobile making an illegal left turn. You advised me to take the car to your collision repair center. I followed your instructions and had the car repaired there. Many parts needed to be replaced. A copy of the repair invoice is enclosed.

Shortly after I picked up my repaired car, I noticed problems in performance. I took the car back to your collision center, but was told there was nothing wrong. I took the car to my own mechanic. He advised me that used parts were placed in my car during the repair process.

I expect to have new, brand name parts used to repair my car. It should be returned to the state it was in before the accident. Please advise when I may return the car to you for these repairs.

Very truly yours,

Michael Motorist
Cc:enc:file

Letter 7: Insurance Claim; Follow-Up for Non-Payment

Robert Rider
12 Bonnie Glen Court
Pasadena, CA 91222
555-555-1010

April 12, 2003

Substandard Insurance Co.
90 Weasel Way
Claremont, CA 91444

Re: Claim #00446581

Dear Sir or Madam:

On March 1, 2003, your insured, Careless Connors, ran a red light and collided with my car. A police officer witnessed the accident. Mr. Connors received a ticket. The court date was April 2. The judge found him guilty on all counts. A copy of the judgment is enclosed.

I submitted a claim to you on March 5. You have not made any attempt to pay this claim for damage to my car for the sum of $1200.00. A copy of the bill is enclosed.

I expect you to remit a check for $1200.00 to me immediately. If I do not receive a check promptly, I shall file a complaint with the state insurance commission. I shall also consider taking legal action.

Very truly yours,

Robert Rider
Cc:enc:file

Letter 8: Credit Life Insurance Assessed on Car Loan

Gullible Buyer
180 S. Hubbard St.
Chicago, IL 60601
773-555-5555

October 13, 2003

Friendly Jack Cars
6700 N. Western Ave.
Chicago, IL 60626

Re: Refund of Sales Charges

Dear Friendly Jack:

On June 5, 2003, I bought a new Asta sports utility vehicle from you. Your salesperson charged me $375.00 for credit life insurance. He stated that credit life insurance was required when financing a car.

Please refund the $375.00 to me and recalculate the loan charges. I now understand that federal law prohibits this charge. The Truth in Lending Act specifically prohibits requiring the sale of credit life insurance in order to secure financing.

I trust that this is an oversight by an uninformed sales person. I expect the revised loan and my check within five (5) business days. A copy of my sales contract is enclosed.

Very truly yours,

Gullible Buyer
Cc:enc:file

Computers

Computers have invaded our lives. They provide entertainment, help us to work more efficiently, and provide information via the Internet. They can also give you a headache when something goes wrong. Software errors (known as *bugs*) are so common that manufacturers post *patches* or *fixes* on their websites for users to download.

Most of us rely on our computers for business and personal use. Having computer access is a necessary part of life in the 21st century. Always buy a product with a warranty. Keep copies of your sales receipts and warranties. These are very important pieces of paper to protect your rights.

Defective Computer Merchandise

Printers and scanners may refuse to cooperate with the computer; software may not perform as promised; and, hardware may fail. Do not spend too much time trying to get yours to work. Send it back for another machine or a credit if you can't get it up and running. Most likely, the machine has defective chips or other technical problems.

Always purchase computers and related items with your credit card. If the product doesn't work, then you can explain the problem to your credit card company and dispute the charge. You won't have to pay the bill if the dispute is resolved in your favor. This gives you some leverage to get the manufacturer to replace the product.

Make certain you shop at a reputable store with a return policy that permits you to return a computer or software once the box or seal is opened. Some stores will not take back software if the box has been opened.

Many of the companies that manufacture these items don't provide a number for customer service. If they do provide customer service, the companies may first ask for your credit card. They have the nerve to charge you for trying to get their defective products to work! Federal and state law may offer some help, depending on the problem.

It cannot be repeated too often: don't pay cash for your purchase. Charge the item on a major credit card so you can refuse to pay if there is a problem.

Internet Service

Internet service providers are a source of frustration for many users. Their security is sometimes lax, allowing hackers to get into their networks and to retrieve personal information. It is often difficult to find a number to call and to speak with anyone in customer service at these providers if you have a problem. Look on the Internet for a help page for your service. You may be able to email a company technician with your problem or call for advice. They make it very difficult for you register a complaint online or to cancel their service. Finding a telephone number to speak with a customer service representative can be quite a challenge. Likewise, it is hard to find an address for communicating by U.S. mail.

If a company is publicly traded, the *Securities and Exchange Commission (SEC)* requires reports that must be filed periodically. The address, telephone numbers, and names of executives are listed in these documents. Find these on the Internet by typing the name of the company and SEC filings into a search engine on the Internet.

High-speed Internet connection services such as DSL are growing rapidly. DSL stands for, digital subscriber line. This is a generic term the telephone companies have given to broadband digital services provided over existing telephone lines. The competition in this consumer market sector is the high speed digital service provided by the cable companies over the existing cable lines. Both provide internet service to your home. Their software may be defective or incompatible with your current computer equipment. Some DSL providers also charge several hundred dollars to connect your equipment to the high-speed link.

Internet Crimes

It is a federal crime to commit certain fraudulent and dishonest acts on a computer or using a computer system. The Department of Justice maintains a website tracking crimes, laws, and other useful information at **www.cybercrime.gov**.

Many states are passing laws to criminalize acts committed in cyberspace. Typical subjects are stalking, adults preying on children, child pornography, and hacking or unauthorized use of a computer system or account. As thieves increase their activities in cyberspace, authorities will extend their reach to protect the consumer's rights.

Never put personal information on an *unsecure* site. Theft may occur even on a supposedly *secure* site. Identity theft is a particularly bad nightmare for anyone caught in this Hitchcock-like dilemma. Your bank accounts can be cleaned out with the a few keystrokes.

Online Purchases

Never pay cash for an online purchase. Always put this purchase on a credit card, not a debit card. This way you have some recourse if the item is not shipped or is defective. Your credit card should not be charged until the item is shipped, but some sellers will charge your card once the order is entered.

An Internet vendor is required to ship an order within the time promised on its website or no later than thirty days after the order is placed, according to the Federal Trade Commission (FTC). If the shipment cannot be sent on time, the vendor is required to notify you of the delay. It must estimate when the product will be sent and ask for your approval of the delayed shipment. You can refuse the extended shipping time and this would cancel your order.

If your purchase does not come as promised, don't wait to contact the seller. Today, many companies have identification numbers for each order that enable you to track the location of your purchase. The Federal Trade Commission has an extensive website with consumer information at **www.ftc.gov**. You may file a complaint online.

Spam (Unwanted Commercial Email)

Is there anyone online today who has not received unsolicited email from vendors who want to sell something? Subscriptions, vacations, cars, dubious drugs, Canadian prescription services, and movie tickets are just a few of the subjects of these unwanted messages or spam.

The United States does not have an enacted law regulating spam, but there are many bills before Congress. Many states currently have anti-spam laws and regulations, including: Arkansas, California, Colorado, Connecticut, Delaware, Idaho, Illinois, Iowa, Louisiana, Maryland, Missouri, North Carolina, Nevada, Ohio, Oklahoma, Pennsylvania, Rhode Island, Tennessee, Utah, Virginia, Washington, and West Virginia.

If you have received spam, complain about it. Send it to your local law enforcement authorities. The Federal Trade Commission (FTC) has a website that enables you to send the spam directly to it at **uce@ftc.gov**. Include the full header of the unwanted message. Another website with useful information about laws regulating spam is located at **http://law.spamcon.org**. Also complain to your Internet service provider. Some providers are able to filter spam.

Taking Action—Step-by-Step

1. Call the customer service number for help. You may not be setting the computer up correctly. Have the representative guide you through the process. If you cannot get a human being on the telephone, or if the manufacturer charges you for this information, ask a *tech savvy* friend to come over to help you get the computer up and running.

NOTE: *Be aware that the customer service representative will often tell you to reinstall the operating system. That is not a very helpful suggestion. Most consumers do not have the ability to run the diagnostic tools shipped with the computer. Some of these customer service centers are there to provide a mere façade of service.*

2. If you still cannot get the machine to work, return it to the seller. If you have followed my advice and charged this on your personal credit card, you can contact the credit card company and refuse to pay the bill. Notify the credit card company that you have returned it to the seller and are disputing the charge.

NOTE: *If you have ordered the computer from an online vendor or a catalog company, be sure to obtain an authorization number from the seller before you ship your equipment back to the seller. The seller may try to avoid giving you this number. Document these problems.*

3. If the seller refuses to take the product back, document the reason. Write down what the seller tells you. Ask a manager to write down the reason you cannot return the product. The store has the right to refuse a return if you did not follow its return policies, such as waiting too long before you return the computer. That being said, many sellers will still take back a defective computer because they do not want unhappy customers.

NOTE: *Computers purchased online or from a catalog should be shipped within 30 days or less. If the item is not in stock, you must receive a message from the seller telling you that it is not available and asking if you wish to cancel the purchase. The seller must tell you when it expects to receive the out-of-stock computer. If your computer does not arrive, then call and write the seller. Refuse to pay your credit card bill if the seller billed your card and you have not received the product.*

4. Complain to the Federal Trade Commission if your merchandise still has not arrived. Complain to the consumer agency in the seller's state and to your local consumer affairs organization. Remember that your state attorney general has a consumer affairs division. Many

states allow you to file complaints online. The Better Business Bureau is a private agency offering dispute resolution. It also has a list of businesses that have many consumer complaints.

NOTE: *Software presents a different problem far worse than the hardware situation. The consumer has very few rights under the seller's shrink wrap license. The retailer may disavow responsibility once you open the package.*

5. Once again, follow my advice. Do not pay cash for computers and software. Using your credit card affords you some leverage. You can refuse to pay the bill. The credit card company may even intervene on your behalf.

Letter 9: Defective Computer

```
Dissatisfied Buyer
18 Grand St.
Cheyenne, Wyoming 09321
888-222-0000


                                August 2, 2003


Horizon Computer Co.
1324 Main Ave.
St. Paul, Minnesota 43422

                            Re: Defective Computer
Dear Sir or Madam:


Please be advised that I recently purchased a new Horizon Ace com-
puter from your website. It cost $2500.00. The computer arrived on
July 31. It does not work.

I am very experienced working with computers. Your customer serv-
ice advice was not helpful. I read the manual and tried all the
suggestions. I believe that this machine has a defective chip.

I am returning the machine to you by commercial shipment. Please
credit my Visa account immediately. A copy of the bill is enclosed.


Very truly yours,



Dissatisfied Buyer
Cc:enc:file
```

Letter 10: Defective Mercandise; Computer Incompatibility

Barbara Black
813 Locust Way
Madison, WI 23490
555-555-5500

May 3, 2003

Big Banana Computers
309 Main St.
Madison, WI 23490

Re: Computer Compatibility

Dear Sir or Madam:

I purchased a Big Banana computer, Model #5698, at your store on April 30. The sales literature states that it is compatible with any printer, including the one I already own.

I have tried to get your computer to work with my existing hardware. It will not. I now understand that I must invest in costly software before your machine will run with my printer.

You should reimburse me for the cost of this software or accept the return of the machine. It does not perform as promised. I have enclosed copies of my receipts for your machine and for the software.

Very truly yours,

Barbara Black
Cc:enc:file

Letter 11: Defective Merchandise; Incompatible Software

```
Internet Subscriber
607 Maple St.
Durango, CO 20202
555-555-5555


                                        May 1, 2003

Customer Service Department
Wild West DSL Provider
P.O. Box 901
Durango, CO 20202

                              Re: Faulty DSL Software
Dear Sir or Madam:


On April 16, I agreed to one year of DSL service. You sent me the
kit to install this service, myself. I am an experienced computer
engineer, however, I cannot install your software because it is
defective and incompatible with the computer I have. When I signed
up for your service, I discussed the type of computer I had with
your representative.


I called your technical support line for help, several times. Your
staff informed me that there are many problems such as I describe.


Please send me new software for my Ace Zip Computers system. I will
not pay the bill for this account #19054 until the service is oper-
able.


Very truly yours,



Internet Subscriber
Cc:file
```

Letter 12: Internet Service; Lack of Security

Frustrated Subscriber
11 Big Street
Austin, TX 00000
310-289-4588

June 8, 2003

Subscriber Services
Wired America Co.
75 Skyscraper Pl.
New York, N.Y. 10009

Re: Hacked Account Complaint

Dear Sir or Madam:

Please be advised that my Internet account was hacked by an intruder on June 7th. I learned of the problem when I tried to access my account that afternoon. I called your customer service number and was told that I could not receive any information because my address was not the address on the account.

This is absurd! The hacker inserted his information for mine. You are trying to verify my account identity with stolen information. Your representative refused to check the billing address previously used or other information that would have correctly identified me. The solution suggested by your representative was to open a new account.

This is the second time within a year that my account has been hacked. Our credit card information was jeopardized on your site. This is also the second time I had to cancel all my credit cards.

The lax security of your service is unacceptable. I cancelled my
account yesterday.

Very truly yours,

Frustrated Former Subscriber
Cc:file

Letter 13: Internet Crime; Stolen Information

Susan Sprocket
25 Sleepy Hollow Dr.
New Buffalo, N.Y. 02345
555-555-5555

                                      January 3, 2003

Manager
All Night Copy Shop
Local College
New Buffalo, N.Y. 02345

                     Re: Stolen Financial Information
Dear Sir or Madam:

On December 2, 2002, I rented time at a computer station in your
store. During that time, I shopped online for holiday gifts.
Shortly after I provided my financial information at your computer,
I learned that unauthorized charges were made to my American
Express account.

I have asked American Express to investigate this matter. At this
time, it is believed that someone gained unlawful access to your
computer system.

Please contact the police to report this cybercrime. I am sure many
other people in your shop were affected, too. Enclosed are the
unauthorized charges.

Very truly yours,

Susan Sprocket
Cc:enc:file

Letter 14: Online Purchase; Shipment not Received

Dissatisfied Buyer
18 Grand St.
Cheyenne, Wyoming 09321
888-222-0000

August 12, 2003

Horizon Computer Co.
1324 Main Ave.
St. Paul, Minnesota 43422

Re: Failure to Ship
Computer

Dear Sir or Madam:

On July 31, 2003, I purchased a Horizon Ace computer from your
Internet site. The price is $2500.00. To date, I have not received
notice of shipment, nor the computer.

I have called your website customer service number without result.

Please advise when the computer was shipped or will be shipped. A
copy of my invoice is enclosed.

Very truly yours,

Dissatisfied Buyer
Cc:enc:file

Letter 15: Online Purchase not Received; Second Letter to Company

Dissatisfied Buyer
18 Grand St.
Cheyenne, Wyoming 09321
888-222-0000

September 5, 2003

Horizon Computer Co.
1324 Main Ave.
St. Paul, Minnesota 43422

Re: Failure to Ship Computer

Dear Sir or Madam:

I purchased a Horizon Ace computer from your website for $2500.00 on July 31, 2003. Despite telephone calls and correspondence to you inquiring about the shipment of the computer, I have not received any information concerning the computer.

Please advise when the computer was shipped and when it will be delivered. A copy of my invoice is enclosed.

Unless I hear from you or receive the computer within ten days, I shall cancel the order.

Very truly yours,

Dissatisfied Buyer
Cc:enc:file

Letter 16: Spam

George Anderson
99 Bosworth Ave.
Durham, N.C. 23000
322-555-1111

May 20, 2003

President
Ace Internet Co.
2200 Skyscraper St.
N.Y., N.Y. 20103

Re: Spam

Dear Sir or Madam:

I have subscribed to your Internet service for two years. During that time, the amount of spam has increased tremendously. The pop-up ads are particularly annoying. The content of the spam emails is very offensive. I do not want to receive sex-related communications.

Please explain the measures you are taking to filter these offensive and irritating messages. For $30.00 a month, I expect you to take care of the customer. There are other Internet services vying for my account. I will consider switching providers unless this problem is resolved.

Very truly yours,

George Anderson
Cc:file

Letter 17: Spam; Violating State Law

Mary Morgan
900 W. Robin Hood Lane
Little Rock, AR 20301
555-555-5555

July 10, 2003

Ridiculous Promises Co.
P.O. Box 88
Goofy, CA 91220

Re: Spam

Dear Sir or Madam:

I am a subscriber to Acme Internet Provider. Your company sends me at least five unwanted emails daily. These communications are lewd and violate Arkansas law and general good taste. Do not send me any more messages.

Arkansas law requires all commercial and sexually suggestive email to be clearly labeled as "ADV-ADULT" in the subject identification line. You must have a functioning email reply and an opt-out method. You must honor the opt-out requests.

I have asked that you stop sending me these messages, but you persist. None of the messages has been labeled as required. Additionally, in further violation of state law, you use false Internet addresses.

This information is being sent to the Arkansas authorities for further action. I have printed all the spam messages you have sent over the past months.

Very truly yours,

Mary Morgan
Cc:file
Cc:Arkansas Attorney General

Employment

Both federal and state laws protect your rights in the workplace. Sexual harassment and discrimination are prohibited. Age, religious, and racial discrimination are not permitted. The *Equal Employment Opportunity Commission (EEOC)* is the federal agency that is responsible for regulating and enforcing the many laws prohibiting workplace discrimination. States and cities often have human rights commissions and labor departments that perform similar tasks.

Discrimination

The main federal law that prohibits discrimination is the *Civil Rights Act of 1964.* It prohibits discrimination in employment based on race, color, religion, sex (gender), or national origin. Under the Act, it is unlawful for an employer to discriminate against any individual in matters of hiring, firing, compensation, terms, conditions, or privileges of employment because of the individual's race, color, religion, sex, or national origin. The Act requires employers to treat members of the opposite sex equally, treat employees of different races equally, and to reasonably accommodate the religious needs of employees.

Legal advice may be available from non-profit groups such as NOW (National Organization for Women), the Anti-Defamation League, AARP (Association for Advancement of Retired People), NAACP (National Association for Advancement of Colored People) and your local bar association. Contact your union if you are a member.

You may also contact the Equal Employment Opportunity Commission or your state labor department for help. The Equal Employment Opportunity Commission website is **www.eeoc.gov**. The website has a link for filing a complaint. You may also contact EEOC Headquarters at:

U.S. Equal Employment Opportunity Commission
1801 L Street, N.W.
Washington, D.C. 20507
202-663-4900

In any case, be aware that the time for filing a complaint and/or lawsuit is very specific. If you miss the deadline for filing, you will lose your right to proceed with your complaint. Depending on the type of discrimination you experience and the applicable law, you may have no more than 180 days after the discrimination occurs to file a complaint with the EEOC. Hiring an attorney is highly recommended.

This is a complex and constantly evolving area of the law. If you think that your rights have been violated, try to document the discrimination. Get the names of people with whom you spoke and any possible witnesses. You should also consult an attorney immediately.

Equal Pay

The *Equal Pay Act* is a federal law that prohibits unequal pay for equal work. Local laws may also be available to guarantee this right. Check with your state and city labor commission, attorney general, and civil rights offices. The law does not require you to file a complaint with the Equal Employment Opportunity Commission before filing a lawsuit.

Mental or Physical Disabilities

Employers with fifteen or more employees are prohibited from discriminating against employees or prospective employees with a known mental or physical disability under the *Americans with Disabilities Act (ADA)*. A *Guide to Disability Rights* is available online at:

www.usdoj.gov/crt/ada/cguide.htm#anchor62335

A person with a disability has 180 days to file a complaint with the Equal Employment Opportunity Commission if an employer has discriminated against him or her. It is advisable to consult an attorney to avoid missing a filing deadline as this is a very complex area of the law. Employers must make reasonable accommodations for disabled workers. Complaints must be filed with the correct agency within a strict time limit.

Age Discrimination

Federal law prohibits age discrimination under the *Age Discrimination in Employment Act*. Workers 40 years and older are protected from discrimination by this federal law. The law applies to companies with twenty or more employees. The law also applies to government agencies. A website explaining the law is at **www.eeoc.gov/facts/age.html**.

Sexual Harassment

Sexual harassment is against the law. Actions of sexual harassment include, but are not limited to placing suggestive pictures in a locker; making lewd comments or gestures; touching or threatening to touch another person in a sexual or threatening way; making sexual advances; leaving pornographic pictures in a locker room; and, other distasteful and illegal acts and comments. If an abusive workplace is created by these actions, then this probably constitutes sexual harassment.

The law used by those filing cases of sexual harassment is usually Title VII of the *Civil Rights Act of 1964.*

Family and Medical Leave Act

Generally, the *Family and Medical Leave Act (FMLA)* is a federal law that requires employers to give eligible employees twelve weeks of unpaid leave to attend to family issues such as the birth of a child, adoption of a child, and family illness. An employee may also use this law to take time off for his or her own serious illness.

The law describes certain requirements for the employee to be entitled to this leave. For example, your employer must have fifty or more employees within seventy-five miles of the worksite. You, the employee, must have worked at least 1250 hours for the employer. For nonemergency leave requests, you must notify your employer at least thirty days in advance of the time you wish to take your leave. You are entitled to have your benefits maintained during your leave, but you must pay for them.

Employee Records

Thirty-nine states allow employees to view their personnel records. The state laws vary widely from free access in California to limited access of only medical records in Ohio. Many states require only public employers to provide access to personnel files.

Illinois has a very liberal policy allowing employees to place a response in their files to evaluations. If possible under your state law, you should periodically review your file. There could be negative information in there that could hurt you. There could also be wrong information in there that could prevent you from being promoted. Correct the records if your state allows this remedy. Contact your state's Department of Labor for more information about the specific laws of your area.

Taking Action—Step-by-Step

1. The employee should go to his or her immediate superior to discuss the problem, if this is practical. If the complaint is about the immediate supervisor, then that is not a good idea.

2. Discuss the problem in a businesslike manner. Provide written documentation if possible.

3. If the first step does not work, then go to your union representative and/or the human resources department. File a formal grievance. If you are a union member, then you may receive free legal help at this point.

4. You may wish to consult an attorney at this point. Learn the specific rules for filing a discrimination complaint in your locality. Federal law requires you to file your complaint within a very specific time frame. If you do not follow the law for filing your complaint, you will lose the right to pursue your case.

5. You may wish to file a lawsuit. Consult an attorney concentrating in employment law as soon as possible. Before you can file a lawsuit based on sexual, racial, or age discrimination, you must file your complaint with the Equal Employment Opportunities Commission.

NOTE: *This is a very complex area of law. Your future is at stake. Try to hire a lawyer if your complaint is not resolved. A lawyer can help you to negotiate a termination package or a settlement of your claim outside of court.*

Letter 18: Race Discrimination; Letter to Human Resources Department

Loyal Worker
Apt. 222
5792 Collins Ave.
Miami, FL 40123
555-555-5555

April 5, 2003

Human Resources Manager
Acme Widget Co.
94 S. Flamingo St.
Miami, FL 40128

Re: Discrimination

Dear Sir or Madam:

On March 28, 2003, I answered your advertisement for factory workers at the main plant. When I arrived to apply for the job, your plant manager refused to give me an application. I asked why he was giving employment applications to others, but not to me. Mr. Snerd, the manager, told me that he had, "bad experiences with my people." He then went on to make several ethnically insulting remarks.

I assume that he denied the application to me because I am from India. You should be aware of the discriminatory practices Mr. Snerd has in hiring employees. I have decided to contact you first to determine if you can resolve this matter to my satisfaction.

If this blatant discrimination is not resolved amicably, I shall be forced to pursue my legal remedies.

Very truly yours,

Loyal Worker
Cc:file

Letter 19: Religious Discrimination; Letter to Direct Supervisor

Observant Jew
8040 DeWitt Clinton Parkway
Brooklyn, NY 22222
212-555-5555

July 11, 2003

Assignment Editor
Newsradio Radio Station
2500 Park Ave.
NY, NY 20200

Re: Work Schedule

Dear Editor:

You have scheduled me to work on Saturdays for the month of September. You are new to this station, so you probably do not know that I cannot work Saturdays, the Jewish Sabbath. I cannot work from sundown Friday until after sundown on Saturday. You should also note that I cannot work on Jewish holidays such as Rosh Hashanah. A list of the holidays and the dates for this year and next is enclosed.

I am available to work other days when my colleagues may prefer not to work. I will be available for work on holidays such as Christmas, Easter, New Year's Eve and Day, plus Sundays. There has never been a problem with this schedule.

You have told me that everyone else at the station works on Saturdays but me. This is because I am the only Orthodox Jewish employee. Federal and local employment discrimination laws guarantee me the right to have my employer respect and accommodate my religious practices.

Very truly yours,

Observant Jew
Cc:enc:file

Letter 20: Unequal Pay

Rosie Riveter
38 Homefront Ave.
Los Angeles, CA 91333
213-343-5555

May 30, 2003

Personnel Manager
Douglas Aircraft Co.
1942 Commercial Blvd.
Los Angeles, CA 91333

Re: Unequal Pay

Dear Sir or Madam:

It has come to my attention that I am paid less than the man next to me on the assembly line. I have worked as a riveter for Douglas Aircraft Co. for $12.12 per hour since the day I was hired, November 1, 2002. The man next to me on the assembly line, Roger Reed, was hired on April 1, 2003, at a salary of $15.00 per hour. He has no experience. I trained him!

Please review my file and adjust my pay retroactively. I am sure that this is an oversight on your part.

Thank you,

Rosie Riveter
Cc:file

Letter 21: Handicapped Accommodation

Mary Reed
84 Lake Tahoe Rd.
Lake Tahoe, CA 90433
555-555-5555

July 3, 2003

Manager
Resort Property Management
35 Circle St.
Lake Tahoe, CA 90433

Re: Handicapped
Accommodation

Dear Sir or Madam:

I am an employee in the accounts receivable department. Recently, I was diagnosed with macular degeneration, a condition that impairs one's eyesight. It can lead to blindness. Right now I am having difficulty seeing the computer screen. There are screens available for visually impaired people.

Please accommodate my visual handicap. I can continue doing my job if I have a computer screen that enlarges the images. These are available through our computer vendor, Geek Guys. The cost is comparable to any other good monitor.

Thank you for your cooperation. A letter from my doctor is enclosed.

Very truly yours,

Mary Reed
Cc:enc:file

Letter 22: Failure to Accommodate Disability; Follow-Up to Manager

Lucille McGillicuddy
623 E. 68th St.
New York, NY 10244
212-247-2099

March 11, 2003

Manager
Delicious Chocolate Factory
84 Bleeker St.
N.Y., NY 20344

Re: Failure to Accommodate Disability

Dear Sir:

Recently, I broke my leg in an accidental fall at home. My doctor has cleared me to return to work, but I need to use a wheelchair. As you know, I am a candy packer on the assembly line. Standing is customary on the line, but I don't believe there is any reason that would prevent me from working while seated in my wheelchair.

I am asking that you accommodate my disability under the Americans for Disability Act and state law. My supervisor has ignored this request. Please contact me to discuss my return to work.

Very truly yours,

Lucille McGillicuddy
Cc:file

Letter 23: Age Discrimination

Ben Borden
18 Maple Dr.
Mayfield, Maryland 66430
404-262-0099

                                        June 11, 2003

Personnel Manager
Reliable Clock Co.
22 Highway 440
Mayfield, Maryland 66433

                                        Re: Lay-off
Dear Sir or Madam:

I have been notified that I am being laid off effective July 1. It concerns me that I am the only person over 40 years of age marked for unemployment. The president of the company told a business magazine recently that the company needed new blood. He also stated that the company had to cut retirement costs.

Employees with far less experience and ability are not being forced to leave. These workers are at least ten years younger than I am. This seems to be age discrimination.

Please contact me to discuss this situation. I prefer to resolve this privately, rather than filing a complaint with a government agency. If necessary, I will be forced to take legal action.

Very truly yours,

Ben Borden
Cc:file

Letter 24: Sexual Harassment; Follow-Up to Human Resources Manager

```
Mary Doll
88 Fantasy L.
Toyland, OR 20044
555-555-0000


                                    March 14, 2003


Human Resources Manager
Ken's Construction Co.
90 E. Dreamhouse Road
Toyland, OR 20048


                            Re: Sexual Harassment
Dear Sir or Madam:


I am writing to notify you that my co-workers at the building site
where I am employed as an electrician are sexually harassing me.
Past complaints to my supervisor have been to no avail.

Enclosed please find a list of offensive incidents and supporting
documentation, including pictures. For example, suggestive notes
have been left in my lunchbox, pictures of nude women and men have
been posted on the inside and outside of my locker, and many rude
remarks have been directed towards me. Some of the men have made
sexual advances towards me, grabbing at me.

I prefer to resolve this privately, but will not hesitate to take
legal action if you do not respond within seven days.


Very truly yours,



Mary Doll
Cc:enc:file
Via certified mail
```

Letter 25: Paternity Leave Request; Follow-Up to Human Resources Department

Ward Cleaver
18 Maple Dr.
Mayfield, America 00022
555-555-5555

April 1, 2003

Vice-President
Human Resources Department
Mayfield Business Corp.
11 Downtown Office
Mayfield, America 00022

Re: Family Leave Request

Dear Sir or Madam:

Please be advised that I plan to take paternity leave from May 15 through June 15. My wife expects to give birth to our first child on May 20. Our company personnel manual provides that fathers are entitled to one month of unpaid leave for the birth of a child.

I have advised my manager of this request, but to date have received no confirmation.

Thank you,

Ward Cleaver
Cc:file

Letter 26: Unpaid Family Leave of Absence

Baby Boomer
900 Cass Ave.
Colorado Springs, CO 33058
555-555-1111

July 10, 2003

Human Resources Manager
Colorado Ski Company
P.O. Box 88
Colorado Springs, CO 33058

Re: Request for Leave

Dear Sir or Madam:

Please be advised that I plan to take a family leave of absence for three months commencing September 1 and ending December 1. My elderly mother needs to have both knees replaced. I need to take care of her during this difficult time. I understand that this will be unpaid leave under the Family and Medical Leave Act.

Thank you,

Baby Boomer
Cc:file

Letter 27: Review Employment Records

Edward Employee
518 Crestview L.
Blue Island, IL 60055
555-555-5555

                                              March 2, 2003

Plant Manager
Big Car Plant
1800 S. Busy St.
Industry, IL 60500

                          Re: Review Employment Records
Dear Sir or Ms.:

I am writing to request the opportunity to view my employment
records of recent performance reviews. My supervisor refused to
give me a copy of the file. I have never requested a chance to see
my personnel records before.

Under Illinois law, 820 ILCS 40/2 (the Personnel Records Review
Act), I have the right to see any information in my employment
records. Please contact me to arrange a mutually convenient time
for me to review my file.

Very truly yours,

Edward Employee
Cc:file

Letter 28: Employee's Statement to be Added to Employment Record

Edward Employee
518 Crestview L.
Blue Island, IL 60055
555-555-5555

March 15, 2003

Plant Manager
Big Car Plant
1800 S. Busy St.
Industry, IL

Re: Employment Records

Dear Sir or Madam:

Thank you for providing me the chance to review my personnel file.

I dispute the accuracy of my supervisor's report on my productivity. We discussed this, but could not agree to remove it from the file. Therefore, I am exercising my right to insert my own statement about this report that I believe reflects the situation more accurately. I understand that state law requires you to place the enclosed statement into my employee file.

I am exercising this right pursuant to 820 ILCS 40/6.

Very truly yours,

Edward Employee
Cc:enc:file

4 Finances

In this age of computers and the Internet, the consumer has one more area in which to be wary. Cyberspace contains new frontiers for the dishonest. Your accounts could be wiped out before you even know it. Your identity can be stolen with a few keystrokes. These new ways to commit theft are in addition to the tried and true methods such as pickpocketing, purse snatching, and fraud. Be aware of your finances.

Do you read the slips of paper with the small print from your credit card company? Do you read the fine print on your bill? You may not know that many credit card companies now require you to submit to arbitration if you have a complaint. Your right to go to court may be limited.

Resolving financial problems often takes several tries. Send letters by certified mail when possible. An alternative method of proving that you mailed a letter is to fill out a Certificate of Mailing at your local post office. This is a small sheet of paper, about the size of an index card, that has the name and address of the sender and the name and address of the recipient. The postal clerk affixes the correct postage and stamps the date of mailing over it. This is proof that you mailed a document. (It is several dollars cheaper than sending letters by certified mail.)

Credit Cards

It is very difficult to function in our society today without a credit card. They can be a great convenience. Credit cards are also a necessity in our e-commerce and mobile society. It is virtually impossible to rent a car or to buy an airline ticket online without a credit card in one's own name. When there are billing errors or problems disputing purchases made with the card, the accounting can turn into a nightmare for the consumer.

Many people pay their bills online. Sometimes those payments disappear into the ether, with the credit card issuer claiming to never have received payment. Your bank account has been debited with the payment, but the company denies it has been paid. Always print out the confirmation page you receive when paying bills online. Do not lose your confirmation number or transaction number—it will help you prove you have paid the bill.

Most credit card companies' necessary information for the consumer to complain is located somewhere in the fine print on the back of the bill. Do not send the letter disputing the accuracy of the bill to the same address for payment of the bill, unless specifically directed to do so. These addresses are often different.

A telephone call to dispute the bill is not effective under the law. The credit card company usually requires that you dispute the item in writing within twenty-eight days or less. Each company has different rules. It is up to you to track down the information.

unauthorized charges

You must dispute the accuracy of a charge on your credit card bill in writing. Be very careful to follow the requirement of your card. The fine print on the back of the bill contains this information. Note that the address to send payments is often different from the address to send complaints and disputes.

Credit cards can be very useful in situations when an unauthorized charge has been made to your card. If a retail company refuses to issue a credit, the credit card company can investigate. You can dispute the bill while the company investigates. During this time period, you do not have to pay the disputed amount.

damaged merchandise

Keep records of your purchases and delivery documents. If merchandise is received damaged and you refuse it upon delivery, write "refused delivery because of damaged merchandise" across the front of the delivery documents. Contact the company to discuss the damaged merchandise. Most companies are reputable and want the customer to be satisfied.

payment processing

Credit card companies have occasionally taken longer than necessary to process payments. This increases the payment of late fees from consumers. If you believe a company is purposely processing your payments late, contact them immediately. Keep track of the amount of time it takes for you to send in a payment and for them to process it.

lost or stolen cards

The minute you know that your card is lost or stolen, or that someone has unauthorized use of the card, call your credit card company to report the situation. You may be responsible for the unauthorized charges if you fail to report the problem promptly.

divorce and credit

This is a very common problem. The credit card company does not care if you are divorced, as long as you are each authorized to use the card. The credit card company does not care what your divorce judgment says about who is responsible for the card; who cannot use the credit card; and, other domestic issues. It is up to the person who's name is on the card to cancel any additional users of the card.

Debit Cards

Debit cards look just like a credit card, but your rights are very different if your card is lost or stolen. Credit card holders cannot be held responsible for more than $50.00 in losses once the card is reported as lost or stolen to the credit card issuer. Debit card holders can lose their entire bank balances to a thief, unless the card is reported lost or stolen with two days. If the bank believes that someone you know used your personal identification number (PIN) to access your account, even if done without your permission, then you can lose the entire sum. The bank can try to hold you responsible for the loss.

If your debit card has been used without your knowledge or permission, fight back! If your complaint letter does not get results, complain to the appropriate consumer or government agency. The *Office of the Comptroller of the Currency* governs national banks. If you are the customer of a national bank, this is the place to take your complaint to the next level.

OCC Customer Assistance Group
Customer Assistance Group
1301 McKinney St.
Suite 3710
Houston, TX 77010
800-613-6743
www.occ.treas.gov/customer.htm

Banks sometimes will try to turn the tables on the customer and accuse the customer of assisting in the theft of the card. Despite being advised not to write down the PIN numbers where they can be found easily, most of us continue to do this. If a dishonest family member finds your PIN, it is still an unauthorized use of the card.

Collecting a Debt

A creditor is permitted to collect its own debts; however, this does not give it license to use abusive collection techniques. Behaviors such as calling the debtor repeatedly at all hours of the day and night; threatening the debtor with jail; and, impersonating a lawyer are prohibited by the *Fair Debt Collection Practices Act.*

The *Fair Debt Collection Practices Act* is a federal law that establishes the guidelines that those trying to collect a debt must follow in their dealings and contact with you. Under the Act, debt collectors must identify themselves as such when they call, and may not contact you before 8 a.m. and after 9 p.m. Also, collectors can not call you at work, if you are not permitted to accept such calls there. They may not call you repeatedly, *nor* harass, oppress, or abuse you. They may not threaten, or use violence to collect a debt. You can instruct a debt collector to not call you again and they must abide by your request. They can still, however, contact you by mail regarding the status of your account.

The Federal Trade Commission enforces this law. Contact them at:

Federal Trade Commission
600 Pennsylvania Avenue, N.W.
Washington, D.C. 20580
877-FTC-HELP (382-4357)
www.ftc.gov/bcp/menu-credit.htm

State and local laws may also regulate debt collectors and their practices. States usually license debt collection agencies, but many of these do not bother to register and cannot legally conduct business in the state. Report these unlicensed agencies.

Credit Reports

You have a right to receive a free credit report if you are turned down for credit or turned down for a job based on this information. You should receive a letter informing you of the reason for your denial if it is based on information from a particular credit-reporting firm. You should also receive information on how to contact the firm for a free report. Send for the report, as many credit reports have errors. You have a right to correct your credit file. Exercise this right.

You can dispute inaccurate information in your credit reports without paying someone to do it for you. The key is that *incorrect* information can be disputed. If the facts in your file are correct, only the passage of time will eliminate this information. Negative credit information stays in your file for seven years. Bankruptcy stays in your file for ten years.

Many websites are available to help consumers. Try your state government resources. For example, the state of New York has a helpful site for consumers wishing to delete negative credit information:

www.consumer.state.ny.us.operationfightback.htm

The FTC has information on its website for those who want to repair their credit at:

www.ftc.gov/bcp/conline/pubs/credit/repair.htm

If you have been denied credit in the past sixty days, you are entitled to a free copy of your credit report. The letter denying you credit should advise you of the name of the credit reporting agency, its address, and telephone numbers. If there is a mistake on your credit file, ask the credit-reporting agency to send you a form for correction. There may be a website that has a downloadable or online correction form. Once you have disputed the information in your file, the company has to delete it if it cannot verify the information.

identity theft

If you have the misfortune of being a victim of identity theft, there are many resources available to help you. The first step you must take is to contact your credit card and debit card issuers and your bank to notify them of the theft. This will limit your liability for charges the thief may make using your credit. Call the telephone number on your cards or your bills given to report a theft. Follow up with a certified letter to the address usually buried in fine print on your statements to report a theft. This provides proof that you notified the creditors and banks of the theft. Keep proof that you mailed the certified letter in your files.

The Federal Trade Commission (FTC) has an identity theft page at **www.consumer.gov/idtheft /fedlaw.htm**. You can complete an *ID Theft Affidavit* online to provide to creditors and police officers. Links to federal debt collection laws and state laws are also listed.

The *Identity Theft and Assumption Deterrence Act of 1998* makes it a federal crime to engage in identity theft. (18 U.S.C. Sec. 1028.) Violations of the act are investigated by various federal agencies, such as the U.S. Secret Service, the Federal Bureau of Investigation, and the U.S. Postal Inspection Service. The Department of Justice prosecutes violators.

Insurance Bills

Open all bills promptly. Ask for an itemized copy of the bill, especially for a hospital visit. If you find errors, dispute the bill as soon as possible. Contact your insurance company to assist you in resolving the problem. The insurance companies have *provider relations departments*. If there are too many complaints by the insured about a particular hospital or doctor, then the company can and does drop them from the managed care provider lists. Often, it only takes a telephone call from the insurance company to one of their contacts to resolve the problem.

Billing errors commonly stem from the health care provider not billing the insurance company correctly. This results in a lower rate of reimbursement. Occasionally, hospitals fail to apply the managed care negotiated discount to the bill. Problems such as these should be addressed immediately.

NOTE: *Check to see if your insurance plan requires dispute letters to be sent by certified mail.*

Investments

The *Federal Securities and Exchange Commission (SEC)* regulates publicly traded stocks, mutual funds, and other securities. The SEC protects investors and maintains the integrity of the market. It regulates stockbrokers and other professionals in the field.

The SEC headquarters is in Washington, D.C. There are regional offices across the country. Consult the main website at **www.sec.gov** to learn the region to which your state is assigned by the SEC. Information about the regional offices is listed on the website. Complaints should be directed to the SEC Complaint Center online or at the address listed below. Complaint forms may be downloaded, but you may also send a letter explaining your problem.

SEC Headquarters
Office of Investor Education and Assistance
450 Fifth Street, NW
Washington, DC 20549
202-942-7040
e-mail: help@sec.gov

SEC Complaint Center
450 Fifth Street, NW
Washington, D.C. 20549-0213
Fax: 202-942-9634

Many investors who are dissatisfied with their returns have filed *arbitration demands*. You should have a lawyer for this process. Many lawyers do not charge a fee unless a recovery is made for you. Look on the Internet or in your telephone book for names of securities lawyers. Many major newspapers and financial dailies carry advertisements offering lawyers' services in this area. Your local bar association and law schools may also have a referral for you.

Investment advisors and stock brokers have a duty to recommend suitable stocks. An elderly, retired person usually needs conservative investments. Clients may state they want high tech speculative stocks. They may be unhappy when the high tech stocks lose most of their value, but that is the risk they took. The broker has not violated the law for placing a speculative stock order if that is what the client wants and the client has been informed that it is a risky stock.

Members of the Military

The *Soldiers' and Sailors' Civil Relief Act of 1940* was enacted to provide protection for members of the military from financial problems while on active duty. (This protection also extends to reservists called to active duty.) The protection includes:

- reduced interest rate on mortgage payments;

- reduced interest rate on credit card debt;

- protection from eviction if your rent is $1,200 or less; and,

- delay of all civil court actions, such as bankruptcy, foreclosure, or divorce proceedings.

The procedure for reducing your interest rate is discussed below. If you find that you are involved in either an eviction or civil action, you can notify the court in which the matter was filed, notifying it of your active status. However, to be sure that the proceedings do not continue without your involvement, contact an attorney.

Those on active duty are entitled to pay no more than 6% interest on their debt. The military member must notify the mortgage company or credit card company of the request to trigger the 6% or less rate. Send a copy of your order requiring you to report to active duty via certified mail. If the military member is out of the country or otherwise unable to write, a spouse, family member, or person with the power of attorney should contact the creditor. A reservist called to active duty should include information about the difference between his or her normal salary and the active duty salary.

The creditor has the right to challenge the 6% interest rate. However, the burden of proof is on the mortgage company or the credit card company to prove in court that the military person is financially unaffected by the call to active duty. Most judges will require the creditor to lower the interest rate to 6%.

This reduction of interest rate is good for all debts incurred prior to military service if the bill is still outstanding. The creditor must reduce the rate to 6% upon receipt of the letter from the military debtor or go to court to prove that the debtor is financially unaffected by the call to active duty. Most creditors will not want to risk a public relations fiasco by challenging a military member's federally guaranteed rights.

The *American Forces Information Service* has a website with detailed information at:

www.defenselink.mil/specials/Relief_Act_Revision

Taking Action—Step-by-Step

1. Keep all your records. Review your statements as they arrive. Monitor your accounts online. There are very definite time limits for reporting forgery or theft to your bank accounts and credit cards.

2. Contact your bank or brokerage. Ask to speak with your personal banker or the branch manager. If there has been theft in your account, then you must call the special telephone number your bank provides. Document the date and time of your call so that you can prove later that you notified the bank of the problem.

3. If the bank employee is not responsive, then ask to speak with a supervisor.

4. Contact the general counsel's office and speak to a lawyer if you cannot get help.

5. Always keep copies of your letters. Send important correspondence by certified mail. Keep records of telephone calls and with whom you spoke.

6. Contact the appropriate government agency next. The Federal Trade Commission monitors credit cards. Bank regulators on the state and federal level may also be of assistance.

7. Consumer lawyers may represent you in a lawsuit for no charge unless you win when you sue a bank or credit card company for various violations.

8. In cases of credit card theft or identity theft, contact the Federal Trade Commission and your local prosecutor. The state attorney general may have an identity theft unit, too. You should also contact your banks and credit card companies. The Social Security Administration should be notified that someone may be using your number.

Letter 29: Credit Card Company; Received Damaged Product

Amanda Beck
915 W. Huron St.
Chicago, IL 60612
773-605-2136

May 1, 2003

Metropolitan Bank Visa Card
P.O. Box 8853
Smalltown, S.D. 82345

Re: Account #909338675

Dear Sir or Madam:

Please be advised that I dispute the accuracy of an item on the May statement, received today. There is a charge for $856.00 for a sofa from Elegant Furniture in Chicago. The sofa arrived ripped in many places. I refused delivery. A copy of the delivery order with "refused because of damage" written across is enclosed. There should be a credit issued for this item by Elegant Furniture.

My account should reflect this fact.

Very truly yours,

Amanda Beck
Cc:enc:file

Letter 30: Credit Card Company; Second Letter, Dispute Charge

Amanda Beck
915 W. Huron St.
Chicago, IL 60612
773-605-2136

June 1, 2003

Metropolitan Bank Visa Card
P.O. Box 8853
Smalltown, S.D. 82345

Re: Account # 909338675

Dear Sir or Madam:

On May 1, 2003, I sent you a letter disputing the accuracy of a charge for $856.00 to my account. This was for a sofa I ordered that arrived damaged. I refused delivery. Elegant Furniture of Chicago should have credited my account for this sum in April.

Please exert some pressure on Elegant Furniture to issue this credit. I also continue to dispute the accuracy of this bill. I am enclosing a copy of my previous letter and another copy of the delivery order.

Very truly yours,

Amanda Beck
Cc:enc:file

Letter 31: Credit Card Company; Error on Statement

Carol Franklin
4433 Main St.
Anywhere, Delaware 02345
555-222-0000

April 2, 2003

Bank of Giant Profits
Visa Card
P.O. Box 1233
Nowhere, S.D. 78943

Re: Error in Billing
Account #3487912

Dear Sir or Madam:

Please be advised that there is an error on my April statement. You have listed a charge to my account from the Corner Table Restaurant in Wilmington, Delaware for $805.00. This is a mistake. I am enclosing a copy of my original charge slip for $8.50. Please correct this error.

Thank you,

Carol Franklin
Cc:enc:file

Letter 32: Credit Card Company; Late Charge Assessed

Amanda Beck
915 W. Huron St.
Chicago, IL 60612
773-605-2136

July 1, 2003

Metropolitan Bank Visa Card
P.O. Box 8853
Smalltown, S.D. 82345

Re: Account #909338675

Dear Sir or Madam:

Please be advised that my July statement contains a late payment fee of $35.00. You assessed this charge because you did not receive my payment until five days after the due date. The payment was mailed 10 days before the due date. The check was presented for payment at my bank one day after the due date. How could you process the check and have it at my bank one day after the due date?

I suspect that, as has been reported in the financial news, you are deliberately failing to process payments in a timely manner. When the customer's check sits on someone's desk for days you can make a handsome profit by charging an undeserved late fee.

I expect that this late fee will be removed and that you will not charge me another fee again.

Very truly yours,

Amanda Beck
Cc:file

Letter 33: Credit Card Company; Unauthorized Use after a Divorce

Careful Consumer
48 Frugal St.
Parsimony, PA 25000
555-888-2222

June 1, 2003

USA Credit Card Co.
P.O. Box 7540
Anywhere, N.D. 90909

Re: Unauthorized Charge

Dear Sir or Madam:

I am writing to inform you of unauthorized activity on my account. All of the charges on May 20 in New Orleans, La. are not mine. My ex-husband, John, made them on a canceled card.

On May 1, 2003, I notified you by telephone and by certified letter that I was canceling charge privileges for my husband, John, effective immediately. We are now divorced. I am not responsible for the charges for the Big Easy Hotel and Bar.

Enclosed please find a copy of the signed, certified receipt for my letter of May 1 and a current telephone and address for my ex-husband.

Please correct the statement.

Very truly yours,

Careful Consumer
Cc:enc:file

Letter 34: Bank;
Unauthorized Transaction on Debit Card

Jane Lostbucks
313 Naylor St.
New Orleans, La. 70113

                                        March 5, 2003

Louisiana National Bank
1 Bourbon St.
New Orleans, La. 70111

                              Re: Debit Card #1234

Dear Sir or Madam:

Please be advised that my debit card with a MasterCard logo was used for unauthorized transactions on December 12 and 13, 2002. Someone was able to access my account to purchase stereo equipment at Joe's Stereo City online on these dates in the amounts of $1200.00 and $500.00, respectively. The store records show that the merchandise was shipped to an address unknown to me. I did not learn of this until my statement arrived yesterday.

I have provided this information to your fraud unit in a telephone conversation yesterday with Mr. Smith.

No one else has access to my card. Please credit my account with $1700.00 to reimburse me for these fraudulent charges.

Very truly yours,

Jane Lostbucks

Cc:file

Letter 35: Bank; Debit Card Used to Empty Checking Account

George Williamson
400 North Ave
Atlanta, GA 70113
555-555-1234

March 7, 2002

Georgia National Bank
1 Peach St.
Atlanta, GA. 70111

Re: Debit
Card #1234

Dear Sir or Madam:

I am writing to advise you that an unauthorized transaction on my debit card emptied my checking account of $2200.00 on 3/3/02. No one has access to my PIN number or card except me.

Please investigate and restore my $2200.00 at once. I learned of this theft when I checked my balance online yesterday. This letter is a follow-up to the telephone call I made to your security office yesterday.

Very truly yours,

George Williamson

Cc:file

Letter 36: Dispute with Bank; Unauthorized Use of Debit Card

George Williamson
400 North Ave
Atlanta, GA 70113
555-555-1234

March 20, 2002

Georgia National Bank
1 Peach St.
Atlanta, GA. 70111

Re: Debit Card #1234

Dear Sir or Madam:

Once again I am writing to insist that you return $2200.00 for an unauthorized debit deducted from my account on 3/3/02. You have declined to restore this sum to my account because I allegedly gave the PIN number or card to someone known to me. This is patently false.

At no time have I shared my PIN number or a card with anyone. It is more likely that a waiter at a restaurant copied my number, or a clerk at a store where I used my debit card memorized my PIN as I punched it in. This is my last demand for restoration of the account. The next step is for me to file a formal complaint with the Office of the Comptroller of the Currency.

I want to resolve this amicably, but will not hesitate to take further action if necessary.

Very truly yours,

George Williamson
Cc:file

Letter 37: Dispute with Collection Agency; Alleged Debt

Constance Coed
19 Campus Dr.
Augusta, ME 13759
333-676-7777

March 16, 2003

Ruthless Collection Agency
900 Mean St.
Elmira, NY 32000

Re: Dispute of Alleged Debt
Your File #313000

Dear Sir or Madam:

I am writing to dispute the accuracy of a debt I allegedly owe to University Credit Card Co. for $502.28. This is incorrect. Please investigate this error and correct your records.

Please do not contact me again in an attempt to collect this debt.

Very truly yours,

Constance Coed
Cc:file
Via certified mail

Letter 38: Collection Agency; Second Letter, Disputing Alleged Debt

Constance Coed
19 Campus Dr.
Augusta, ME 13759
333-676-7777

March 29, 2003

Ruthless Collection Agency
900 Mean St.
Elmira, NY 32000

Re: Dispute of Alleged Debt
Your File #313000

Dear Sir or Madam:

This is the second time in a few weeks I have been required to write to you to dispute the accuracy of an alleged debt. On March 16, I notified you by certified mail that I disputed the alleged debt and that I did not want to be contacted again by you to collect this contested debt. A copy of the March 16 letter is enclosed.

On March 28, I received another collection letter from you. Once again, I am stating that the I dispute the accuracy of this alleged debt and that I do not want to be contacted again by you in any manner in an attempt to collect this sum.

You have violated the Fair Debt Collection Practices Act by persisting in your efforts to collect this debt. I shall take any further violations very seriously, including pursuing my legal remedies.

Very truly yours,

Constance Coed
Cc:enc:file
Via certified mail

Letter 39: Credit Agency; Negative Credit Report

```
Alan Trainspotter
25 Alumni St.
Iowa City, IA 34090
555-555-1212


                                           March 19, 2003


Big Credit Agency
P.O. Box 88
Arlington TX 50899
                                       Re: Errors in File


Dear Sir or Madam:

T was recently turned down for a car loan. The letter denying my
loan stated that your agency has negative credit information about
me. Please send me my free copy of this report. My social security
number is: 000-00-0000. A copy of the letter is enclosed.


Thank you,



Alan Trainspotter
Cc:enc:File
```

Letter 40: Credit Agency; Errors in Credit Report

```
Alan Trainspotter
25 Alumni St.
Iowa City, IA 34090
555-555-1212


                                     March 30, 2003


Big Credit Agency
P.O. Box 88
Arlington TX 50899

                              Re: Errors in File
Dear Sir or Madam:


I have reviewed a copy of my credit report from your agency. Please
note that this does not appear to be my account. This information
belongs to another gentleman with the same last name, but a dif-
ferent spelling of the first name, "Allen," a different social
security number, and a different birthday.


Please correct these errors immediately.


Very truly yours,



Alan Trainspotter
Cc:file
```

Letter 41: Insurance Billing Error

Paul Patient
3389 W. Maple Dr.
Tucson, AZ 86432
444-890-9999

May 8, 2003

Patient Accounts Manager
Local Hospital
200 Gold St.
Hot Town, AZ 86433

Re: Billing Error/Account #30943

Dear Sir or Madam:

I received your bill for my hospital stay of March 11-13. It was not itemized. Please send me a detailed statement including each and every charge made to me for this stay. Until I see the detailed bill, I cannot be certain, but I believe that you have charged me the wrong rate.

My managed care plan has negotiated substantial discounts with your institution. You have apparently charged me the full rate, instead of the discounted amount. I have compared your bill with that paid by my insurance company.

Please correct your bill.

Very truly yours,

Paul Patient
Cc:file

Letter 42: Hospital; Second Letter, Insurance Billing Error

Paul Patient
3389 W. Maple Dr.
Tucson, AZ 86432
444-890-9999

June 3, 2003

Patient Accounts Manager
Local Hospital
200 Gold St.
Hot Town, AZ 86433

Re: Billing Error #30943

Dear Sir or Madam:

Once again I am writing to you about a billing error for my hospital stay in March. I have disputed this bill previously in my correspondence to you dated May 8. A copy of this letter is enclosed.

To date you have not provided a detailed bill. Once again, I dispute the accuracy of your charges. Based on the insurance payments and explanation of benefits provided to me by my managed care insurance company, I believe that you have charged me the full rate. I should have been charged the discounted rate negotiated by my insurance company.

Please correct this error. I am still waiting for an itemized bill.

Very truly yours,

Paul Patient
Cc:enc:file

Letter 43: Liquidation of Brokerage Account

Jane Investor
4 Easy Street
Palm Springs, California 00000
123-123-4567

August 11, 2002

Dewey Fleeceum and Howe
Investment Company
18 Main St.
New York, New York 11111

Re: My Brokerage Account

Dear Sirs:

I am writing to advise you that I am closing my account with you immediately. Please liquidate my holdings and send the check to my new broker, Mr. Honest Broker.

You knew that I am a retired widow on a small social security and pension income. Still, you managed to invest in speculative funds that caused a loss in my IRA account in the past six months from $180,000 to $90,000 or a loss of 50% of the value.

You placed me in inappropriate investments for someone my age and in my financial situation.

Very truly yours,

Jane Investor
Cc:file

Letter 44: Follow-Up Letter to Securities Exchange; Liquidation of Brokerage Account

Jane Investor
4 Easy Street
Palm Springs, California 00000
123-123-4567

September 15, 2002

Securities and Exchange Commission
Headquarters
450 Fifth St., N.W.
Washington, D.C. 20549-0213

Re: Broker Complaint

Dear Sir or Madam:

I am writing to complain about the conduct of my broker, Dewey Fleeceum and Howe. On August 11, 2002, I sent the firm a letter requesting that my IRA account be closed and the funds sent to my new broker immediately. To date I have not received any response.

The Dewey firm invested inappropriately for me causing a loss of 50% of the value of my account in six months. I have enclosed a complaint form that I downloaded from your Internet site.

Anything you can do to help me to get the balance of my funds from Dewey would be greatly appreciated. Copies of the correspondence are enclosed.

Very truly yours,

Jane Investor
Cc:enc:file

Letter 45: Securities Exchange Commission; Reporting Brokerage Violations

John Investor
22 North Ave.
Providence, RI 12345
101-333-8644

April 18, 2003

Securities and Exchange Commission
Headquarters
450 Fifth St., N.W.
Washington, D.C. 20549-0213

Re: Brokerage Violation

Dear Sir or Madam:

I am writing to you to complain about self-dealing by my brokerage house and stockbroker, Cheatum and Scarum.

On July 1, 2002, I opened a brokerage account at Cheatum and Scarum. I deposited $350,000.00 that represented my retirement savings. I explained to the broker when I opened the account that I needed to carefully and conservatively manage this money. I also explained this in writing at the time I opened the account.

Almost from the moment I opened the account, I received calls from my broker, Jeffrey Lying, touting one stock or another. He claimed that in-house research recommended these "hot" stocks. Mr. Lying invited me to lunch on many occasions and after several drinks, I agreed to invest in his recommended stocks. These stocks were losers. I lost over half the value of my investment in a short period of time.

Imagine my shock when I read the financial pages and learned that the big stock brokerage houses were paid to recommend certain stocks. They promoted stocks while privately selling their own interests in these companies.

I am enclosing copies of the trades in my account. Please investigate.

Very truly yours,

John Investor
Cc:enc:file

Letter 46: Credit Card Company; Reduction in Interest Rate due to Military Service

Amanda Beck
230 Cresthill Circle
Great Lakes, IL 61300
847-555-5050

June 30, 2003

Avarice Credit Card Co.
P.O. Box 1185
Sioux City, IA 24550

Re: Military Relief
Account #995577

Dear Sir or Madam:

Please be advised that I am a member of the U.S. Navy on active duty since March 1 of this year. The interest rate on my credit card account is 20% APR. While serving my country on active duty, I am requesting that you charge the 6% per year interest rate to which I am entitled by the Soldiers' and Sailors' Civil Relief Act of 1940.

My bill should be adjusted to reflect the 6% interest rate retroactively to March 1. A copy of the order calling me to active duty is enclosed.

Thank you,

Amanda Beck
Cc:enc:file

5 Health

There are many new federal and state laws that have been enacted in response to consumer complaints regarding health care. Federal law requires new privacy measures by health care providers to protect your right to privacy. The smart consumer needs to be informed about these changes.

Insurance companies may try to avoid paying for expensive medications and procedures. Do research to support your request for treatment. If your request is denied, you must file a written appeal conforming to your insurance company's procedures. Enlist the aid of your doctor to write a letter explaining the need for the treatment.

There are state insurance regulators that have consumer complaint departments. State attorneys general may also have consumer health complaint divisions. These public servants intercede on your behalf to persuade the insurers to reconsider the denial of coverage. Insurance companies can be fined and/or have their licenses to do business in the state revoked.

People without health insurance coverage should be aware of federal laws that require hospitals receiving federal funds to provide free care under certain circumstances. This could provide a safety net for those not covered by a public aid plan or Medicare. No one can be turned away from an emergency room for inability to pay or lack of coverage. The emergency room personnel cannot even ask you about insurance until after you have been evaluated.

Keep copies of all medical bills, receipts, and claim forms. Do not send original documents to the insurance company unless required. Retain all statements from the insurance company that show claim activity and payments on your behalf known as *explanations of benefits*. (Most insurers do not keep records of this activity, so you cannot get a copy at a later date.)

Health Insurance Portability and Accountability Act (HIPAA)

The *Health Insurance Portability and Accountability Act of 1996 (HIPAA),* as amended, provides strong privacy protections for patients effective April 14, 2003. Your medical information and records must be kept confidential. The doctor, hospital, or other health provider cannot disclose any information about you without your written permission.

Each health care provider must provide a privacy notice to you by mail or in person at your first visit after April, 2003. The provider must designate a *privacy officer*, to address any complaint of privacy violations. Keep a copy of this notice when you receive it. A copy of the federal law, HIPAA, may be obtained from the Office for Civil Rights. The website is **www.hhs.gov/ocr/hipaa**.

The *Department of Health and Human Services* is a federal agency that enforces HIPAA. The *Office of Civil Rights (OCR)* is a special division that investigates complaints. Anyone can file written complaints with OCR by mail, fax, or email. There are ten regional offices. Check the website **www.hhs.gov/ocr/privacyhowtofile.htm** to see the region to which you belong. Help is also available at the Office for Civil Rights at 800-368-1019.

The complaint must be addressed to the correct Regional Manager and must:

- be filed in writing, either on paper or electronically;

- name the entity that is the subject of the complaint and describe the acts or omissions believed to be in violation of the applicable requirements of the Privacy Rule;

- be filed within 180 days of when you knew that the act or omission complained of occurred. (OCR may extend the 180-day period if you can show *good cause*.); and,

- have occurred on or after April 14, 2003 (on or after April 14, 2004 for small health plans)—for OCR to have authority to investigate.

Office for Civil Rights
U.S. Department of Health and Human Services
200 Independence Avenue, S.W.
Room 509F, HHH Building
Washington, D.C. 20201
800-368-1019
OCRMail@hhs.gov

Billing Errors

Insurance companies and doctors can *and* do make billing errors. For instance, the doctor's office may not put the correct name of the doctor on the insurance claim form. If the office makes a claim in the name of the practice group, "Prairie State Physicians," instead of the individual physician's name, "Jane Doe, MD," it may be rejected as out-of-network. Conversely, your insurance company may have your doctor listed under the group name. A claim submitted under the individual doctor's name could be rejected. Your claim could be denied or paid at a much lower rate. This is a very common problem.

Another place for error is in the coding of the illness and treatment by the health care provider. Each illness and procedure has a diagnostic code. The wrong code can mean that your claim is not paid or paid at a fraction of the cost.

Medical providers do not issue itemized bills very often. Anyone who has been hospitalized recently has not received a detailed bill. Most of us never even see the bill. It goes directly to the insurance company. We are only contacted when the insurance company does not pay the full amount of the bill.

Prescription Drug Coverage Refusal

When paying for prescriptions, many managed care insurance companies follow a list of authorized drugs called a *formulary*. The company makes a list of frequently prescribed drugs and then obtains generic or discount prices for the medication. If the drug you need is not listed in the formulary, payment will be denied routinely. However, you can challenge this refusal to pay.

Ask your doctor to contact the medical director of the insurance company. This is often information unavailable to the policyholder, but it is available if you do some research. Check business publications, public documents, the state insurance department, and with your local reference librarian.

Identify the drug you want to have covered. Describe how it is used to treat your illness. Cite any studies showing the effectiveness of this drug. Using this information and a letter from your doctor, challenge the denial. Just because it is not on the formulary does not mean that you cannot benefit from it. This is especially true if you have a rare illness.

It is imperative that you follow the insurance company requirements for appealing the denial of your coverage. There are usually very strict time requirements for requesting an appeal after being denied coverage. Time may be on your side if you are trying to receive a new drug or treatment. The insurance company may be evaluating covering a drug if medical practice accepts this new treatment. Should the insurance company deny coverage for this drug, ask about covering it under the major medical part of your plan. Sometimes this provides a loophole for coverage.

Do not hesitate to contact your state department of insurance for help. Some state attorneys general also have health care assistance available. A letter or call from a government regulator can be very effective. Save this for last. Try the other avenues of assistance first. If time is critical for treatment, do not hesitate to obtain government assistance. (See Appendix C for information on specific state insurance regulators.)

Denial of Coverage

There are some expensive medications and types of surgery and procedures that are typically not covered by insurance companies. For example, weight reduction surgeries, breast reductions, and fertility treatments are often not covered unless a state law requires it. You must dispute any denial of coverage in writing according to the rules of your insurance company. There are usually strict time limits in which you can appeal.

The cooperation of your physician is crucial. You will need a letter from your doctor along with the pertinent medical records. If surgery is involved, you need a letter from the surgeon describing the procedure and the need for the surgery.

Today, most insurance companies have websites. Go to your insurance company's website. Many of them have treatment guidelines on the Internet. These are intended for doctors to review treatments. Sometimes clerical personnel will reject a claim for coverage even when the company's medical guidelines cover the surgery. If the company lists your surgery and states the circumstances it will pay for the operation, you should print out this information. Determine whether you meet the guidelines for treatment.

Research your case. Do Internet research through Medline plus (**www.nlm.nih.gov/ medlineplus**) about your illness or condition. Sometimes the insurance company is unaware of new studies or medications. If you and your doctor can show the company the facts substantiating the desired treatment, you may get the company to pay for it.

Uninsured Patient

The *Hill-Burton Act* authorizes assistance to public and other nonprofit medical facilities such as acute care general hospitals, special hospitals, nursing homes, public health centers, and rehabilitation facilities in the form of federal funding. In return for federal funds, the facilities may not deny emergency services to any person residing in the facility's service area on the grounds that the person is unable to pay for those services. The Act does not require the facility to make non-emergency services available to persons unable to pay for them.

The Act further requires the health care facilities that receive Hill-Burton funds to make services provided by the facility available to persons residing in the facility's service area without discrimination on the basis of race, color, national origin, creed, or any other ground unrelated to the individual's need for the service. The website for this information is operated by the federal agency for Health and Human Services at **www.os.dhhs.gov/ocr/hburton.html**.

County hospitals often provide care on a sliding scale or for no charge for those without insurance. University hospitals may also be able to offer care at reduced rates. Ask for a social worker to assist you in finding funding or applying for public assistance such as Medicaid.

Hospital Accreditation

Contact the head nurse immediately if you have a dirty room. He or she can call the housekeeping department to send someone up to clean the room. You may also be transferred to another room that is in better condition.

Many larger hospitals have a hospital ombudsman to assist patients in resolving conflicts within the hospital. The ombudsman acts as the patient's advocate with the administration. Ask if there is an ombudsman.

Inform your doctor about the problems at the hospital. Call his or her office and leave a message that you want to be called, even after office hours. The doctor should know what is happening. He or she can call a hospital administrator to fix the problem. Also, most doctors practice at more than one hospital. The doctor should be advised of the problems so that he can choose to admit his patients to another hospital.

The state and trade groups must accredit hospitals. The state health department may regulate hospitals in your state. Ask for the name of the agency that supervises hospitals if the state health department does not in your state. An industry group, the *Joint Commission on Accreditation of Healthcare Organizations* inspects and monitors hospitals. Without accreditation, a hospital will close. Complaints may be sent to:

Office of Quality Monitoring
JCAHO
One Renaissance Boulevard
Oakbrook Terrace, IL 60181
630-792-5636
E-Mail: complaint@jcaho.org
www.jcaho.org

Nursing Homes

Nursing homes may soon be serving two generations of baby boomer families: elderly parents and their aging children. The quality of care in these homes ranges from superb to abominable. Money alone does not guarantee proper care. Relatives of nursing home patients must be vigilant. Do not be complacent. Investigate the home before a family member is placed.

State health departments monitor the quality of patient care in nursing homes. All states have an office of aging staffed with ombudsmen to help seniors with nursing home and skilled care facility problems. Look for information for your state on the Internet at **www.cms.hhs.gov/contacts /contactlist.asp**. Another excellent website is the *National Citizen's Coalition for Nursing Home Reform* at **www.nccnhr.org/static_pages/help.cfm**. The organization is located at:

1424 16th Street, NW
Suite 202, Washington, D.C. 20036.
202-332-2275
Fax: 202-332-2949

Health Care Power of Attorney and Living Wills

People are entitled to decide what kind of medical care and extraordinary measures they want in the event of a catastrophic illness such as an accident, stroke, aneurysm, heart attack, or other life threatening conditions. Each state and the District of Columbia have laws recognizing one's right to decide his or her fate (*living will*) and to appoint an agent to direct the medical care if the patient is physically and/or mentally incapacitated (*healthcare power of attorney*). The laws and forms for each state vary. Some states have a uniform living will and durable power of attorney for healthcare. Other states have their own forms and requirements. The documents provide an outline of powers, but not every situation is covered.

A good website to visit for more information on this topic is:

www.ama-assn.org/public/booklets/livgwill.htm

choosing the right person

The person who has been selected to be the agent for the power of attorney should be advised of the responsibility. The person should be asked if he or she wants to serve. The person making the appointment should discuss this with the agent well ahead of the time it might be needed. Make certain that this person will follow your instructions and beliefs and not his or her own. Some people do not want to be responsible for another's life, so pick a friend or a relative who knows you and your wishes and is comfortable with the responsibility. The agent designated for the healthcare power of attorney should have a copy of the living will and the power of attorney.

When you are hospitalized, the admissions office will ask for a copy of the healthcare power of attorney and living will or for the name of the person holding these documents for you. Let friends and family know if you will be undergoing surgery or will be admitted to the hospital. If you have these documents prepared and available, your wishes must be honored.

Pharmacy/Prescription Complaints

Each state has a department to regulate pharmacies and pharmacists. Contact your state agency for more information and/or to file a complaint. The following website has links to each state's agency:

http://userpages.umbc.edu/~ycoles1/consumer_pharmacy_frame1.htm

Some managed care companies often require patients to use mail order pharmacies. That makes it difficult to talk to a pharmacist. Orders are sometimes lost. Drugs are sent from different locations around the country once your prescription is entered and you could wait weeks for your order. If you need your medication, you have to pay full price at a local pharmacy. If this happens to you, save your receipt. Contact your insurance company and insist that they reimburse you for this expense.

Fair Debt Collection Practices Act

Laws are available to provide relief from abusive debt collection under the federal *Fair Debt Collection Practices Act.* The Fair Debt Collection Practices Act is a federal law that establishes the guidelines that those trying to collect a debt must follow in their dealings and contact with you. Under the Act, debt collectors must identify themselves as such when they call, and may not contact you before 8 a.m. and after 9 p.m. They may not call you repeatedly, nor harass, oppress, or abuse you. They may not threaten to, or use violence to collect a debt. You can instruct a debt collector to not call you again and they must abide by your request. They can still, however, contact you by mail regarding the status of your account. (See Chapter 4 for a more information.)

Taking Action—Step-by-Step

1. First, discuss the problem with your doctor. If this is a hospital or nursing home problem, speak with the head nurse. There may be a patient advocate or ombudsman whose job is to assist patients with hospital bureaucracy and problems.

2. If this does not resolve the problem, contact the head of the hospital or the nursing vice-president. State your problem concisely and always keep records.

3. If you have a billing problem, contact the head of the patient accounts department.

4. If the safety of a patient is the issue, file a complaint with the regulatory agency that licenses doctors, nurses, or hospitals in your state. Nursing home problems should be reported promptly to the state agency or local health department. States are required to have an agency to assist senior citizens. Many local agencies exist to help seniors. Contact these agencies for help. They can be quite effective.

5. For a privacy complaint, contact the privacy officer. The doctor, hospital, or other health provider must give you this information. The privacy officer should try to resolve the complaint. If not, file a complaint with the federal Department of Health and Human Services.

Letter 47: Doctor's Employees Violated Privacy Act

John Doe
10 Pleasant St.
Sick Bay, Ohio 11111
456-123-4567

July 1, 2003

Privacy Officer
Family Doctor, M.D.
4 Medical Center Dr.
Get Well, Ohio

Re: Violation of Privacy

Dear Privacy Officer:

Please be advised that I am filing a formal complaint with you concerning a violation of my right to privacy granted by the federal Health Insurance Portability and Accountability Act of 1996 (HIPAA).

On my recent visit for diabetic care at your office the following problems occurred:

1. Your receptionist called my name in the waiting room and asked me the reason for my visit in front of the entire room.

2. Your receptionist then proceeded to use the intercom to call the nurse to advise her that "a diabetic" checked in.

3. The nurse opened the door from the back offices into the waiting room; called my name and said, "It is time to check your blood sugar."

4. While waiting to see the doctor in an examination room, my file was placed in a pocket on the door with my name and reason for my visit prominently displayed.

5. On my way out, the receptionist stated loudly that I needed to
   return to see the doctor in three weeks to check if my diabetes
   was under control. She also read off my insurance coverage and
   stated the balance I owed in front of the entire waiting room.

These incidents humiliated me. I do not wish to share my personal
information with anyone other than those necessary.

Please address these issues.

Very truly yours,

John Doe
Cc:file

Letter 48: Doctor's Office; Second Letter, Concerning Violation of Privacy

John Doe
10 Pleasant St.
Sick Bay, Ohio 11111
456-123-4567

July 15, 2003

Privacy Officer
Family Doctor, M.D.
4 Medical Center Dr.
Get Well, Ohio 40800

Re: Violation of Privacy

Dear Privacy Officer:

I have not yet received any information from you about my rights under the new federal law effective April 14, 2003. Please send me a copy of your privacy notice for patients.

Thank you,

John Doe
Cc:file

Letter 49: Department of Health; Follow-Up Letter, Violation of Privacy

John Doe
10 Pleasant St.
Sick Bay, Ohio 11111

August 15, 2003

Secretary
The U.S. Department of Health and Human Services
200 Independence Avenue, S.W.
Washington, D.C. 20201

Re: Violation of Privacy

Dear Secretary:

I have tried to resolve various violations of my rights to medical privacy under HIPAA with my doctor without success. Enclosed please find a copy of my letter of July 1, 2003 to the privacy officer at Dr. Friendly's office. I have not received a reply.

Please investigate my complaint.

Thank you,

John Doe
Cc:enc:file

Letter 50: Health Insurance; Billing Error

Jane Patient
4 Maple Dr.
Skokie, IL 62700
847-555-0000

                                              May 3, 2003

Oak Healthcare Co.
Member Services
1 Corporate St.
New York, N.Y. 11111

                                  Re: Member Number 1234

Dear Sir or Madam:

Please be advised that a billing mistake was made in processing
payment for the enclosed bill from my physician, Dr. Michael
Feelgood. You have paid him as an out-of-network provider, but he
is a member of the network of physicians in my plan. He practices
with the St. Elsewhere medical group at the address on the enclosed
bill.

Please review the payment of this claim. I should not have any liability for payment, except for the $15.00 co-payment I already
made. You should have paid Dr. Feelgood at 100% reimbursement
instead of the 70% rate.

Thank you for your prompt attention to this matter.

Very truly yours,

Jane Patient
Cc:file

Letter 51: Health Insurance; Refusal of Prescription Drug

Robert Outofpocket
6 Nomeds Lane
Soothe, Virginia
55555
434-400-1234

April 2, 2003

Oak Healthcare Co.
Member Services
1 Corporate St.
New York, N.Y. 11111

Re: Member #458921

Dear Sir or Madam:

On March 22, 2003, you processed my claim for payment of Cellsept, a prescription drug. Payment was denied because it is not in your formulary.

I suffer from a very rare illness, Behcet's Disease, which requires the use of this new drug. A letter from my physician supporting this statement is enclosed. There is no other drug available for treatment of this condition.

Please review the denial of payment for this drug.

Very truly yours,

Robert Outofpocket
Cc:enc:file

Letter 52: Health Insurance; Second Letter, Reconsider Refusal of Prescription Drug

Robert Outofpocket
6 Nomeds Lane
South, Virginia
55555
434-400-1234

April 22, 2002

Oak Healthcare Co.
Member Services
1 Corporate St.
New York, N.Y. 11111

Re: Member #458921

Dear Sir or Madam:

I am writing to you to request that you reconsider the denial of payment for my medication, Cellcept, a new prescription drug. This drug is not in your formulary, but my doctor wants me to have this new pill. A letter from my physician, Dr. John Doe, is enclosed.

Please contact me at the address above, if you need more information.

Very truly yours,

Robert Outofpocket
Cc:enc:file

Letter 53: Health Insurance; Claims Clerk Error

Amanda Veranda
12 Lafayette Pl.
New Orleans, La. 72110
505-333-2222

July 15, 2002

Dr. Aaron Ace
Medical Director
Cheap Insurance Co.
3478 Smith Dr.
Suite 1100
Cleveland, OH 223344

Re: Member #7777

Dear Sir or Madam:

I am writing to request that your company reconsider its refusal
to pay for my medication, Remicade. This drug is given in the doctor's office or hospital via intravenous line. Payment for
treatment has been denied because your claims clerk stated that
pills are available at a lower cost for the treatment of my rheumatoid arthritis.

Enclosed please find a letter from my physician summarizing all the
drugs I have already tried without much success. Remicade is a new
drug that is proving very useful in treating cases of rheumatoid
arthritis that have not responded to other drugs.

Please reconsider the denial of this treatment. I need it desperately.

Very truly yours,

Amanda Veranda
Cc:enc:file

Letter 54: Health Insurance; Denial of Coverage

John Jones
18 Brummel St.
Evansville, IN 82304
555-555-1212

March 23, 2003

Medical Director
Tight Fisted Health Organization
1200 Main Highway
Indianapolis, IN 82300

Re: Surgery Appeal

Dear Doctor:

I am writing to you to appeal the denial of coverage for my requested stomach stapling procedure. My internist has written to advise that I am 50 years old, diabetic, and 125 pounds overweight. You declined to pay for this surgery because it is cosmetic.

My internist, Dr. Stuart Sonshein, and my surgeon, Dr. Nancy Craft, believe that this operation is medically necessary. I enclose their documentation.

Your treatment guidelines available on the company website clearly state that those who are more than 100 pounds overweight qualify for the coverage of this surgery. I believe you denied coverage for me in error.

Please reconsider your denial of this surgery.

Very truly yours,

John Jones
Cc:enc:file

Letter 55: Hospital; Uninsured Patient

Uninsured Patient
18 Hardluck St.
Philadelphia, PA 02222
555-555-5555

July 14, 2003

Patient Accounts Manger
Franklin University Hospital
12 Freedom Sq.
Philadelphia, PA 02222

Re: Uninsured Patient

Dear Sir or Madam:

I do not have health insurance because I was laid off from my job over a year ago. My benefits have run out.

On June 5, I was injured in a car accident. I needed surgery and was hospitalized for four days. I recently received a bill for $100,000.00. I called your office to ask about the rates for care. Your representative told me that patients without insurance are billed at a premium rate.

You receive federal and state funds and are obligated to provide care for the needy under certain circumstances. I believe that you should reduce the bill to the discounted amount paid by managed care insurance.

Please send me an itemized copy of the bill.

Very truly yours,

Uninsured Patient
Cc:file

Letter 56: Hospital;
Unclean Facilities and Poor Care

Kirby Katt
929 Westgate Dr.
Albuquerque, NM 04020
555-444-9898

June 3, 2003

President
Local Hospital
25 SW St.
Albuquerque, NM 04022

Re: Unclean Facilities
and Poor Care

Dear Sir or Madam:

I was hospitalized at your facility on May 28-30. I was in Room 422.

The room was dirty when I arrived. Used towels and washcloths were in the bathroom. I called the nurse, but no one came to clean. I called housekeeping, but no one responded. My doctor arrived for rounds and saw the mess. When she addressed the staff, finally someone cleaned and provided fresh linens.

The dietary department never came so that I could order food. I did not eat for 24 hours because I was told I was not on the computer list. Each mealtime I called the dietary office and the nurse, but I was told the food was on the way.

Please contact me to discuss these problems.

Very truly yours,

Kirby Katt
Cc:file

Letter 57: Nursing Home; Lack of Acceptable Care

Baby Boomer
38 Mockingbird Lane
Onarga, IL 60300
555-555-1455

May 15, 2003

Administrator
Superior Nursing Home
14 Montebello Dr.
Lincoln Way, IL 60305

Re: Mother Boomer's Care

Dear Sir or Madam:

My mother, Betty Boomer, is a patient in your facility. She suffers from advanced Alzheimer's disease.

When I visited my mother recently, I was shocked to see that she had bedsores, her linens had not been changed, and her clothes had not been changed. It was obvious that no one had bathed my mother in some time. I rang for help, but no one came.

Finally, I went to the nurse's station to complain. No nurse was there. An aide told me that the buzzer system had been broken for several weeks. She also confided that they were very short of staff.
This lack of care is unacceptable and dangerous. Please contact me to discuss this matter at once. I enclose a copy of my mother's power of attorney giving me the right to handle her affairs.

Very truly yours,

Baby Boomer
Cc:enc:file

Letter 58: Hospital; Life Support for Relative

Ann Adams
330 E. Lake Shore Dr.
Chicago, IL 60600
312-555-5555

April 23, 2003

President
University Hospital
2000 University Center
Chicago, IL 60699

Re: Life Support for Leonore Adams

Dear Sir or Madam:

I am a daughter of Ann Adams, a patient at your hospital. My mother has been a patient at your hospital for several weeks after suffering a stroke. Her condition is poor, but according to the doctors, there is hope.

The doctors say that life support is available, but not recommended for my mother. I believe that she would want to fight for life at all costs. I know that I want her to have every available opportunity to live.

My brothers and sisters do not agree with me. Please have the doctors start my mother on life support immediately.

Very truly yours,

Ann Adams
Cc:file
Via hand delivery

Letter 59: Hospital;
Power of Attorney for Healthcare

Jane Adams
2588 McHenry Sq.
Marengo, IL 60000
815-555-5555

April 24, 2003

President
University Hospital
2000 University Center
Chicago, IL 60699

Re: Life Support
for Leonore Adams

Dear President Cook:

Thank you for your letter concerning life support for my mother, Leonore Adams. I understand that my sister, Ann, has contacted you to demand that life support be initiated for our mother immediately.

Please be advised that I hold the Power of Attorney for Healthcare and Living Will for my mother. Copies of these documents are enclosed. You will note that my mother did not want to have any extraordinary means used to prolong her life in the case of a stroke or other catastrophic event. We talked about this many times. She watched others suffer and lose their dignity during prolonged, unsuccessful hospitalizations.

My sister, Ann, has been estranged from the family for some time. She has not even spoken with my mother in years. My mother knew that I would respect her wishes, even if the decision is painful. Please place a "do not resuscitate order" (DNR) on my mother's chart.

Very truly yours,

Jane Adams
Cc:enc:file

Letter 60: Mail Order Pharmacy; Dispute Charges and Service

Marsha Monroe
894 Wilshire Blvd.
Beverly Hills, CA 90210
213-555-5555

April 12, 2003

Customer Service Manager
Budget Mail Order Pharmacy
P.O. Box 1200
Las Vegas, NV 22222

Re: Acct. 36322

Dear Sir or Madam:

I am required to use your pharmacy service by my insurance company. The quality of care is very poor.

As a diabetic, I need to have a constant supply of my insulin and other medications. You have lost my orders or denied that I requested the prescriptions. I am often required to place the same order two or three times, before it is sent. Many times I have run out of medication because of your mistakes. Then I am required to fill the prescriptions at a local pharmacy at a much higher rate. I am enclosing those higher rate prescriptions for reimbursement.

The prescriptions have been short of pills prescribed. My most recent order of Prandin contained 76 pills instead of the 90 that were ordered and charged to my account.

If this service does not improve, I shall complain to the state and federal authorities. I have already complained to my insurance carrier.

Very truly yours,

Marsha Monroe
Cc:enc:file

Letter 61: Collection Agency; Cease Contact

Uninsured Patient
18 Hardluck St.
Philadelphia, PA 02222
555-555-5555

July 24, 2003

Ruthless Collection Agency
P.O. Box 600
Johnstown, PA 02300

Re: Cease Contact
Your File: #3080

Dear Sir or Madam:

Please cease and desist from contacting me to collect a debt allegedly owed to the Franklin Hospital for $100,000.00. I am disputing the accuracy of the debt. In any event, I do not wish to be contacted again about this matter.

Very truly yours,

Uninsured Patient
Cc:file
Via certified mail

Home

Landlord/tenant questions are very common. How you can get your security deposit back, when your landlord can withhold the security deposit, and whether a landlord is required to accept a *Section 8* (government housing assistance voucher) tenant or not are all answered in this chapter. There are, however, other issues having to do with your home that are covered here as well.

For example, home buyers need to know that they cannot be forced to carry *Private Mortgage Insurance (PMI)* under certain circumstances. If the home owner has 20% or more equity in her home she cannot be required to continue to carry this insurance by the lender.

Another subject covered is cable installation in your home. If you are stood up for a cable appointment, you can ask to be reimbursed—in some cities—for the time you lost in waiting for someone to show up to install your cable.

This chapter also includes an extensive explanation of the Do Not Call Registry, the wildly successful federal program to prevent solicitors from calling you at home. The rules of each state are included. Information about where to sign up is provided.

If debt collectors calling your home is driving you crazy, you can stop them in their tracks by knowing the law you will learn here. All you have to do to stop the calls is to inform the collection agencies that you do not want to be contacted again. This chapter explains how to do this.

And, finally, for members of the military, this chapter discusses your rights while on active duty. Your mortgage rate cannot exceed a certain amount, no matter what your mortgage note says. Your credit cards cannot exceed a certain interest rate despite what your credit card company tries to charge.

Safety Conditions

Property owners have a general duty to keep their premises free from hazards. An accumulation of ice on stairs required to access the apartment is possibly negligent. State laws vary about the liability for shoveling snow. For example, in some states, the landlord is protected if he or she does not shovel the natural accumulation of snow and ice. However, if the landlord chooses to remove the ice and/or snow and does it negligently, he or she may be liable for injuries.

The tenant should file the insurance claims. Always keep copies of the hospital bills and records. Send all correspondence and claims certified mail. If the injuries are serious enough, consider retaining an attorney. Consult a lawyer if you have a slip and fall case. Lawyers usually do not charge for personal injury suit consultations. They will collect a fee from the defendant if the case is successful.

Home Improvement

Contracting for home repairs and improvements can be a risky venture. Most contractors and service providers will not begin working until a deposit is made or perhaps until an entire contract is paid in full. This leaves the consumer in a position of not being able to hold back payment for unsatisfactory, untimely, or incomplete work.

If you are in a situation where you have paid for work in-full prior to actually having it completed, you have a few choices to resolve a problem of unsatisfactory work. If the company does not respond to your written complaint, you have the option of complaining to your local Better Business Bureau. The Better Business Bureau works to facilitate communication between the company and the consumer—to help both sides come to a satisfactory resolution to the complaint. It also keeps records of business that have had complaints filed against it. However, the Better Business Bureau does not have authority over the company and does not take sides in disputes.

Going to Small Claims Court is another option. Small Claims Courts are generally available in every state to resolve disputes, where the amounts in questions are small. The actual amounts that can be brought in Small Claims vary by state, but generally have a maximum range from $2500 to $5000. Small Claims Courts are designed to be used without an attorney, so as to move quickly and more informally. Generally, there will be court costs and fees involved in just filing your suit.

Beyond these remedies, there may be other local or statewide consumer advocacy groups that can help. Check with your local government offices or your state Attorney General's office to learn if additional remedies exist for your situation.

cable television laws

In addition to the federal laws governing cable television, local laws may regulate your cable television company. Consumers have complained of missed service calls to their local lawmakers. As a result, many areas enacted laws that require the cable company to pay penalties to the subscriber for missed service calls and broken appointments. Check your local laws. Call your town or city for a copy of the laws in your area. Ask your local reference librarian for additional help.

utility lines

Utility companies can be sued for negligence. The homeowner has a right to have the requested service performed in a reasonable and careful manner. The utility company service should stake out the entire property. The purpose of calling the utility service to mark the spot where the utility lines run before digging is so no damage will be done. The homeowner has the right to be fully compensated for any damage caused by this kind of negligence. It is entirely foreseeable that a failure to mark utility lines can result in damage to the property.

If the utility company agent that was supposed to survey the property and stake out the utility lines was negligent, an insurance claim should also be filed with the homeowner's insurance company and the utility company. It wouldn't hurt to contact a local council member or state representative about the utility problem. The local public utility board should be notified, too.

Housing Discrimination

The Department of Justice administers the *Fair Housing Act*. It is illegal for housing providers to deny housing based on race, color, religion, sex, national origin, familial status (children under the age of 18 or a pregnant woman), or disability. Housing providers include landlords and real estate companies as well as other entities, such as municipalities, banks or other lending institutions, and homeowners insurance companies. It is also illegal to refuse to rent or to sell a house to a person with a disability, a family with children, and a person with HIV/AIDS or related illnesses. It is illegal to refuse to make certain accommodations for people with recovering from alcohol and substance abuse or HIV/AIDS-related illnesses.

Some local laws prohibit discrimination on the basis of source of income. *Section 8* is a housing program for low-income people. In Chicago, it is discrimination to refuse to rent to a Section 8 tenant simply because the source of the rent payment is federal funds. Local laws vary, so it is probably best to consult an experienced landlord/tenant lawyer. Landlord associations or tenant advocacy groups may also have helpful information.

Federal laws prohibiting discrimination on the basis of source of income are enforced by the *Department of Housing and Urban Development (HUD)*. The agency's website is at **www.hud.gov**. The website is extensive. There is an online complaint form. You may also obtain a copy of the complaint form and mail it in or drop it off at a local office. The addresses and telephone numbers of regional offices are also available on the website. The national address is:

451 7th St., S.W.
Washington, DC 20410
202-708-1112

Security Deposits

Most state and local laws require the landlord to return the security deposit if the apartment is clean and without damage, except for normal wear and tear. Usually the landlord is required to provide an itemized list of repairs and paid bills to justify the withholding of the security deposit.

It is advisable to take pictures of the way in which you leave the premises if you are a tenant. You should also try to obtain an inspection of the apartment by the landlord when you move out so that you have a written record of the condition in which you left the premises.

Private Mortgage Insurance (PMI)

Most lenders require borrowers to have *Private Mortgage Insurance (PMI)* in case the borrower defaults on the loan. The *Homeowner's Protection Act* requires lenders to automatically terminate private mortgage insurance (PMI) at certain scheduled dates under certain specific requirements. It also allows for borrower requested cancellation at certain scheduled dates. The Act applies to loans made after July 29, 1999, and excludes certain high risk FHA and VA loans.

In general terms, borrowers may request that PMI be cancelled when the principal balance of the mortgage loan reaches 80% of the original value of the property securing the loan. If the home-owner does not request cancellation, PMI is to automatically terminate when the loan balance, based solely on the amortization schedules for the loan, reaches 78% of the original value of the property securing the loan.

If you signed a mortgage before July 29, 1999, you may ask your lender about canceling the PMI if you have 20% or more equity in your home. Federal law does not require your lender to cancel the PMI.

Freddie Mae and *Freddie Mac* are organizations that buy mortgages from lenders. They have regulations governing the payment of PMI. Individual states may have laws that regulate the payment of PMI. Contact your state consumer protection agency or attorney general for more information for your particular situation. (See Appendix A for detailed information concerning your state's attorney general.) The Federal Trade Commission (FTC) enforces the rules about the sale of Private Mortgage Insurance (PMI). The website for this agency is:

www.ftc.gov/ftc/consumer.htm

If you have PMI, carefully monitor the balance of your loan. If your property has appreciated greatly, you may wish to get an appraisal to prove that you have more than 20% equity in your home. The reasoning behind the imposition of PMI is that lenders believe that an owner with little equity is more likely to default on the loan.

Do Not Call Registry

The federal Do Not Call law is regulated by the Federal Trade Commission (FTC). The FTC maintains a national *Do Not Call Registry*. Registration is free. Consumers may sign up to be listed to prevent telemarketing calls by either a toll free number or online as of July 1, 2003. Telemarketers will have access to the list as of September, 2003. They must delete the names of those who have asked to be listed in the registry at least every ninety days. Registration is good for five years. To register online, go to **www.donotcall.gov**. You may also register by calling 888-382-1222. You must call from the telephone number you wish to place on the Do Not Call list.

Most telemarketing calls should stop within three months after you are registered. There are some businesses that are exempt from the law: telephone companies and airlines and other common carriers, banks, credit unions, and insurance companies. However, telemarketing companies often make telemarketing calls for exempt businesses. The telemarketing companies must comply with the *Do Not Call* registry, even if they are calling on behalf of exempt businesses.

The *Telephone Consumer Protection Act* does not cover political solicitations. Telemarketers calling on behalf of charities do not have to remove your name from their list, but you can direct the charity itself to strike your name from its telephone list. The charity cannot have a telemarketer call you after your request.

Even if you have registered your name on the national list, the law permits companies that have an established relationship with you to call for up to eighteen months after your last purchase, delivery, or payment to it. You can ask the company not to call again, but if the company continues to call despite your request, it may be fined $11,000.00. If you make an inquiry at a company or send in an application, the company can call you for three months afterward.

NOTE: *There are state and federal do not call lists. There may be additional penalties for violating a state do not call law. Check with your state. (See Appendix A for information to contact your state's attorney general.)*

NOTE: *As we go to press, a federal court has ruled that Congress did not give the Federal Trade Commission (FTC) the authority to enforce the law for violations of the Do Not Call registry. Members of Congress have promised to pass immediate legislation giving the FTC the authority the judge felt it lacked; thus overruling the court opinion. Check the author's website at:* **www.101complaints.com** *for the status of the registry and more information for consumers.*

Spam

Spam is a real problem for most computer users. The Federal Trade Commission (FTC) has estimated that 86% of addresses posted to websites and to newsgroups receive spam, and that 50% of addresses posted on free personal websites receive spam. Internet providers are trying to filter the unwanted commercial emails, but many emails still get through.

The Federal Trade Commission (FTC) enforces spam laws. You may file a complaint by forwarding the spam directly to the FTC at **uce@ftc.gov**. You may also use the complaint form online by going to the consumer website for the FTC at **www.ftc.gov**. There are links to these forms. The toll free telephone number is 877-FTC-HELP. Contact it for specific regulations in your own state. A website that lists each state law regarding spam is:

www.spamlaws.com/state/summary.html

Delay in Shipment

The seller must notify you if the goods cannot be shipped within a reasonable period of time. Your credit card should not be charged until the goods are shipped or expected to be shipped. You must be told that the order cannot be sent and given the option to cancel or to wait for the merchandise to ship. This is called a *delay notice*. The Federal Trade Commission regulates this transaction.

fair credit billing act

The *Fair Credit Billing Act* permits you to dispute the credit card bill if your order is not received. You must notify the credit card company in writing within sixty days of receiving the bill with the error. Send the letter certified mail so that you can prove when it was mailed. You do not have to pay the bill during the time you are disputing the charge. The Federal Trade Commission has a website addressing this issue at **www.ftc.gov/bcp/conline/pubs/credit/billed.htm**.

Soldier's and Sailor's Relief Act of 1940

This federal law provides active duty military personnel with certain rights and financial benefits. A creditor cannot charge a military member more than 6% interest per year. This is true for mortgages, student loans, credit cards, car loans, furniture purchases and other consumer loans—even those made before the call to active duty or joining the military.

You must notify the creditor of your call to active duty. It is recommended that you enclose a copy of your orders or other proof of your duty status. If you are a reservist, you may wish to send a copy of your civilian pay stub and the reservist active duty pay stub to prove the disparity in your income. Send a copy of your orders to your creditor company via certified mail. If your orders are secret, then get a letter from your commanding officer or the base legal department stating that you have been ordered to active duty. The lender must lower your interest rate as requested immediately.

The creditor can go to court to try to prevent the lower interest rate. This presents another dilemma because under the Act, members on active duty are immune from service of process and cannot be forced to go to civil court. It is unlikely that a creditor will challenge this law by refusing to lower the interest rate as directed. However, should a problem arise, military personnel should ask their base legal officer for assistance. Local bar associations may be available to assist you at no charge.

Letter 62: Tenant Injured on Rental Property

Jane Tenant
Apartment 10
1800 Ridgeway
Wilmette, IL 60091
847-256-1212

January 16, 2003

Landlord Properties Management
190 W. Randolph
Chicago, IL 60602

Re: Slip and Fall

Dear Sir or Madam:

I am a tenant in an apartment managed by your firm in Wilmette, Illinois. On the evening of January 6, I slipped on accumulated ice and snow on the outside back staircase leading to my apartment from the parking lot. All the lights in the area were burned out.

It had been snowing for several days, with several cycles of thawing and freezing. No one shoveled the snow or made any attempt to remove the ice. There was no salting done in the area. The sidewalk and stairs were very slippery as a result.

I slipped on the icy steps and fell down the steps, landing on my back, and hitting my head on the pavement. I am enclosing the emergency room bills and subsequent medical bills incurred as a result of the fall.

Please report this incident to your insurance company. I prefer to resolve this without litigation, but will not hesitate to retain an attorney if this is not settled quickly and amicably.

I expect to hear from you within 10 business days.

Very truly yours,

Jane Tenant
Cc:enc:file

Via Certified Mail
Return Receipt Requested

Letter 63: Carpet Company; Contract Terms not Honored

Craig Tully
9436 E. 12th St.
New York, N.Y. 20122
213-555-1212

February 1, 2003

Gotham Carpets, Inc.
333 Amsterdam Pl.
N.Y., N.Y. 20122

Re: Carpet Installation

Dear Sir or Madam:

On December 1, 2002, I signed a contract to purchase new, wall-to-wall carpeting from you to be installed at my apartment before Christmas. I was assured that you could order the carpet and install it before the holidays. As you can see by the enclosed copy of the contract, I stated clearly that installation must be completed prior to December 24, 2002.

The job was started on December 18, but not completed until January 15, 2003. I called; wrote; and, visited your showroom to inquire about the lack of progress—but could not receive satisfaction.

I believe that you should refund $500.00 of the purchase price because you breached our agreement. It was very important to me to have that carpet in before I entertained family and friends in my home. Instead of receiving compliments on my new décor, I had to warn guests not to trip over the rolls of carpet and mats piled all over my home. This was not the decorating scheme I had in mind.

Please refund $500.00 to me to end this matter.

Very truly yours,

Craig Tully
Cc:enc:file

Letter 64: Cable Company; Missed Appointment

Cable Subscriber
14 Monterey Dr.
Chicago, IL 60600
773-404-1212

June 12, 2003

Cable TV Company
1111 W. State St.
Chicago, IL 60601

Re: Failure to Keep Scheduled Appointment

Dear Sir or Madam:

This is to notify you that your service representative failed to appear at the scheduled appointment in my home on June 1, 2003 at 10 A.M. I waited until 2 P.M. and no one from your company came or called. I took the day off from work to be home when your company was supposed to install our cable system.

Under local law, I am entitled to be paid for a missed appointment. Please credit my account as required.

Very truly yours,

Cable Subscriber
Cc:file

Letter 65: Utility Company; Failure to Mark Utilities

Linda Homeowner
22 Charm St.
Winnetka, IL 60090
847-555-0000

May 1, 2003

Utility Clearinghouse
7345 Maple Ave.
Evanston, IL 60201

Re: Failure to Mark Utilities

Dear Sir or Madam:

Please be advised that I called your office to advise that I needed you to send out a crew to mark the utility lines in my front and back yards. We planned extensive landscaping. We needed to know where the utility lines were buried to avoid disturbing them.

On April 30, you sent a crew to mark the buried lines. However, only the front yard was marked. The back yard was never marked and the landscaper cut all utilities buried in the back including, electricity, cable, computer access, telephone, and gas. I was out of town for the day. I was not happy to return home late that night to learn of this disaster.

I called your JULIE service in order to prevent this kind of damage. There is no excuse for this. Please contact me so that we can discuss a settlement of my damages without litigation.

Very truly yours,

Linda Homeowner
Cc:file

Letter 66: Real Estate Company; Discriminatory Practice—Race

Home Buyer
90 Cobbled Road
Old Tyme, CT 40034
555-555-1212

May 2, 2003

Manager
Prejudiced Realty Co.
100 Main St.
Fancy Town, CT 40085

Re: Discriminatory Practice

Dear Manager:

I am interested in purchasing a home in your lovely town. In April, I telephoned your office to inquire about seeing homes for sale. The realtor on floor duty was assigned to assist me. I made an appointment with that realtor, Joe Blow, to show me various properties. He faxed the listing sheets to my office prior to the appointment on April 30.

When my wife and I arrived at your office to meet the realtor, he became very upset and flustered. Mr. Blow told us that all the places he wanted to show us had been sold in the past day or two. He suggested that we look in another area in which we had no interest. I believe that Mr. Blow decided not to show us these homes because we are black. He was unaware of our race until we met in person at your office.

This had nothing to do with our finances. I already own a home in the community. I am a partner in a business consulting firm and my wife is a physician in this community. I called the listing brokers for the properties we were told had been sold. The brokers informed me that this was not true.

Please contact me to discuss this situation. I plan to file a complaint with the proper agencies given the seriousness of this discriminatory practice.

Very truly yours,

Home Buyer
Cc:file

Letter 67: Rental Company; Refusal to Rent—Children

Rose Renter
Apt. 860
2200 W. Grand
Town, NH 01222
555-555-8999

April 8, 2003

Apartment Rental Management
P.O. Box 203
Town, NH 01222

Re: Discriminatory Practice

Dear Sir or Ms.:

On April 5, 2003, I visited your open house to inspect apartments for rent. I liked your model apartment and asked for a rental application. The manager on duty refused to give me an application when he learned I am the single mother of two children, ages 8 and 10. This is discrimination.

The Fair Housing Act is a federal law that prohibits discrimination against prospective renters based on factors including familial status, among others. You cannot refuse to rent to me just because I am a single mother of two young children.

Please reconsider renting to me. Perhaps your manager made a mistake. I trust you do not have a corporate policy that refuses apartments to families with children. I prefer to resolve this issue directly with you, but I will pursue other legal remedies if necessary.

Very truly yours,

Rose Renter
Cc:file
Via Certified Mail

Letter 68: Property Management Company; Return of Security Deposit

Former Tenant
2 Greenbay Rd.
Kenilworth, IL 60033
847-256-1212

April 20, 2003

Landlord Properties Management
190 W. Randolph
Chicago, IL 60602

Re: Return of Security Deposit
1800 Ridgeway, Apt. 10
Wilmette, IL

Dear Sir or Madam:

Please return my security deposit of $750.00, plus interest. I vacated my apartment at the end of March in compliance with my one-year lease. The apartment was clean and in good repair, less normal wear and tear. Your rental agent, Mary Jones, walked through the vacated apartment with me and signed the checklist stating that the premises were left in good condition. I am enclosing a copy of the signed checklist.

I am certain this must be an oversight in your bookkeeping. Now that I have reminded you of this, please return the security deposit, plus interest, to me at the above address.

Thank you,

Former Tenant
Cc:enc:file

Via Certified Mail,
Return Receipt Requested

Letter 69: Bank;
Cancel Private Mortgage Insurance

Betty Beisner
3065 Tranquil Drive
Muscatine, Iowa 20649
222-555-6788

May 5, 2003

Mortgage Department
Big Bank of Iowa
600 Main St.
Muscatine, IA 20649

Re: Cancellation of PMI

Dear Sir or Madam:

Please cancel my Private Mortgage Insurance on loan #09213 for my home. The loan was signed on 10/12/98. I have been a good customer; never missing a payment. I have about $25,000 remaining on the original $125,000 loan. The property is currently valued at $250,000.

Thank you,

Betty Beisner
Cc:file

Letter 70: Bank;
Cancel Private Mortgage Insurance

John Homeowner
22 Wistful Vista
Anytown, U.S.A.
200-555-5555

July 1, 2003

Bank of U.S.A.
Mortgage Lending Department
1200 Columbus Drive
Kansas City, KS 67388

Re: Loan #34909

Dear Sir or Madam:

I signed a mortgage for the purchase of a single-family home with you on August 3, 1999. The original mortgage amount was $100,000.00. I now have paid the loan down to $80,000. The home is currently appraised at $375,000.00. There is more than 20% equity in my home.

Please cancel the Private Mortgage Insurance (PMI) on this property.

Very truly yours,

John Homeowner
Cc:file

Letter 71: Bank; Second Letter to Cancel PMI

John Homeowner
22 Wistful Vista
Anytown, U.S.A.
200-555-5555

July 15, 2003

Bank of U.S.A.
Mortgage Lending Department
1200 Columbus Drive
Kansas City, KS 67388

Re: Loan #34909

Dear Sir or Madam:

On July 1, 2003, I wrote to you requesting the cancellation of my Private Mortgage Insurance (PMI) since my home equity exceeds 20% of the original property value. You have failed to do so.

The Homeowners Protection Act of 1998 permits a borrower to cancel the PMI once the home equity is 20% or more.

Please cancel this PMI. I trust that I do not have to take further legal action.

Thank you,

John Homeowner
Cc:file

Letter 72: Company;
Remove Customer from Call List

Gerald Jones
3030 N. Utica St.
Albany, N.Y. 00000
1-234-555-8888

April 11, 2003

Ms. Nancy Pick
President
Ace Aluminum Siding Co.
28 Main St.
Schenectady, N.Y. 02345

Re: Do Not Call List

Dear Ms. Pick:

I am writing to direct you to add my name to your "Do Not Call List." I have also registered with the New York State list asking that telemarketers refrain from calling me at home.

Please make this addition to your list immediately. If I continue to receive telephone solicitations from your company, I shall take further action.

Very truly yours,

Gerald Jones
Cc:file

Letter 73: State Do Not Call Registry; Report Violation

Gerald Jones
3030 N. Utica St.
Albany, N.Y. 00000
1-234-555-8888

August 15, 2003

New York State Consumer Protection Board
Do Not Call Complaints
5 Empire State Plaza
Suite 2101
Albany, N.Y. 12223-1556

Re: Do Not Call

Dear Sir or Ms.:

On August 5, 2003, I received a telemarketing call from Ace Aluminum Siding Co. despite the fact that I signed up for the state registry in April, 2003. The call came at approximately 2 P.M. from a telemarketer who identified himself as, "Joe Jones." The tele-marketing firm placing the call is Universal Annoyance Inc., a New York corporation.

Please investigate my complaint. The completed form is enclosed.

Thank you for your prompt attention to this matter.

Very truly yours,

Gerald Jones
Cc:enc:file

Letter 74: Federal Do Not Call Registry; Report Violation

Alexandra Bell
10 Oak St.
Cincinnati, OH 02468
888-555-1212

October 1, 2003

Federal Trade Commission
Do Not Call Registry
600 Pennsylvania Ave. N.W.
Washington, D.C. 20580

Re: Violation of Do Not Call List

Dear Sir or Ms.:

On June 28, 2003, I registered my telephone number on the Do Not Call List with your office. I received online confirmation of my registration. Despite being listed, I received a telemarketing call from Annoying Calling Company about switching my long distance carrier. This call was received at my home on October 15, 2003 at about 8 P.M. The caller gave his name as Joe Blow. The caller i.d. showed the following number: 555-888-1212.

Please investigate this call.

Very truly yours,

Alexandra Bell
Cc:file

Letter 75: Internet Service Provider; Spam Problem

I.M. Connected
3085 Internet Highway
Silicon Valley, Ca. 91203
714-348-9521

May 1, 2003

Internet Service Provider
1200 Green St.
St. Louis, Mo. 63188

Re: Spam Complaint

Dear Sir or Madam:

I am writing to complain about the vast quantity of vile spam I receive in my email account with you. Although I have complained numerous times online, you have failed to respond to my concerns. The spam is as troublesome as ever.

If you cannot filter the unwanted and offensive email, then I shall be forced to switch to a provider than can.

Thank you for your prompt attention to this matter.

Very truly yours,

I.M. Connected
Cc:file

Letter 76: Internet Provider; Second Letter, Cancel Service

I.M. Connected
3085 Internet Highway
Silicon Valley, Ca. 91203
714-348-9521

May 15, 2003

Internet Service Provider
1200 Green St.
St. Louis, Mo. 63188

Re: Spam Complaint

Dear Sir or Madam:

On May 1, 2003, I wrote via U.S. mail notifying you of my dissatisfaction with the spam I receive in my email account. The sheer quantity of advertising and pornographic messages clogs my email. I am required to spend hours each week erasing and blocking the unwanted messages.

Once again, you have ignored my requests to contact me to discuss a resolution to the spam attacks. As a result, I am cancelling my subscription, immediately. I am switching my Internet Service Provider to a company that uses filtering software to block the spam.

Very truly yours,

I.M. Connected
Cc:file

Letter 77: Internet Advertiser; Delete Name from Email List

I.M. Connected
3085 Internet Highway
Silicon Valley, Ca. 91203
714-348-9521

May 5, 2003

Obnoxious Advertiser
890 Commercial Ave.
Orlando, Florida 23904

Re: Spam Complaint

Dear Sir or Madam:

Please delete my name from your email list: imconnected2@cool-mail.com. I have already made this request online several times without result. I no longer want to receive any communication from you. If you fail to remove my name from your list, I shall have no choice but to file a formal complaint with the Federal Trade Commission.

Thank you,

I.M. Connected
Cc:file

Letter 78: Federal Trade Commission; Internet Advertiser, Refusal to Remove Name from List

```
I.M. Connected
3085 Internet Highway
Silicon Valley, Ca. 91203
714-348-9521


                                            May 20, 2003


Federal Trade Commission
600 Pennsylvania Ave., N.W.
Washington, D.C. 20580

                                            Re: Spam


Dear Sir or Madam:


I am writing to complain that the Obnoxious Advertising Co. has
failed and refused to remove my name from its online subscription
list despite numerous requests. Enclosed please find my complaint
form printed from your internet consumer site.


Please require the company to remove my name.


Very truly yours,



I.M. Connected
Cc:enc:file
```

Letter 79: Catalog Order not Received

Catalog Shopper
250 Fifth St.
Milwaukee, WI 53009
203-353-8650

July 10, 2003

Lovely Lingerie Co.
19 Simpson St.
Indianapolis, IN 64033

Re: Order not Received

Dear Sir or Madam:

On June 12, I ordered several items from your summer catalog—order
#180347. To date I have not received any of the items.

Please advise as to when I should expect this merchandise.

Thank you,

Catalog Shopper
Cc:file

Letter 80: Catalog Company; Second Letter, Order Information

Catalog Shopper
250 Fifth St.
Milwaukee, WI 53009
203-353-8650

July 25, 2003

Lovely Lingerie Co.
19 Simpson St.
Indianapolis, IN 64033

Re: Order Not Received

Dear Sir or Madam:

On July 10, I wrote to you about your failure to deliver my order of June 12—order #180347. A copy of this letter is enclosed. I still have not received any of the order. You have not notified me of a reason for delay of this shipment.

I am sure that this is an oversight on your part. Please do not endanger my otherwise pleasant customer relationship with your company. Send my order or notify me of when it will be shipped.

Thank you,

Catalog Shopper
Cc:enc:file

Letter 81: Catalog Company; Third Letter, FTC Violation

Catalog Shopper
250 Fifth St.
Milwaukee, WI 53009
203-353-8650

August 5, 2003

Lovely Lingerie Co.
19 Simpson St.
Indianapolis, IN 64033

Re: Order not Received

Dear Sir or Madam:

I have written to you twice concerning your failure to deliver my order of June 12—order #180347. Copies of the two previous letters are enclosed.

Despite my two previous requests, you have failed to either ship the merchandise or to notify me of the reasons for the delay and when the order will be shipped. This is a violation of the Federal Trade Commission rules.

If you cannot ship the merchandise; notify me at once. Otherwise, I expect to have the items in my hands within a week. If you continue to ignore my requests, I shall take further legal action. Remove my name from your customer lists. I would never buy anything again from your company after this shabby treatment. As a customer of 20 years standing, I expected a better business relationship.

Very truly yours,

Catalog Shopper
Cc:enc:file

Letter 82: Mortgage Company; Second Letter, Reduce Mortgage Interest Rate for Military

Military Homeowner
80 Cherry Dr.
Onarga, IL 68900
555-555-2525

March 25, 2003

Customer Service Manager
Friendly Mortgage Co.
P.O. Box 249
St. Louis, MO. 63111

Re: Loan #69094

Dear Sir or Madam:

On March 15, I wrote to inform you that I am a member of the military called to active duty. I enclosed the necessary paperwork with that letter. Once again I enclose the copies of the paperwork and a copy of my letter because you have not responded to my request that the interest rate on my mortgage be lowered to 6% or less.

You are an FHA lender. Under the Soldier's and Sailor's Relief Act of 1940, you are required to advise me of the adjusted amount due, provide adjusted coupons or billings, and see that the reduced amounts are not refused as insufficient payments.

The April payment is due shortly. I expect to hear from you immediately upon receipt of this letter.

Very truly yours,

Military Homeowner
Cc:enc:file

7 School

Students with physical, mental, and emotional disabilities are often *mainstreamed* (sent to class with other children). They are not always sent to different schools or classrooms as may have occurred in the past.

More and more children are being diagnosed with disabilities from Attention Deficit Disorder to Dyslexia. Each one of these children is entitled to a good education. The school must accommodate the student's disabilities. This may mean anything from tests without time limits to a personal aide for the student.

Federal and state laws govern the treatment of children with disabilities in the school. The parents or guardians of these children must be their advocates to insure that all the services required are provided by the school. In special circumstances, if the school cannot accommodate the child's needs, then the district must pay the cost of another school for the child—even sending the child to an out-of-state boarding school.

Individual with Educational Disabilities Act

The *Individuals with Educational Disabilities Act (IDEA)* requires schools to identify and provide special education to students with special needs. Once a child has been identified as in need of special education services, the school must prepare an *Individualized Education Plan (IEP)* within thirty days. Specialists such as the child's teacher, school psychologist, special education consultant, social worker, and others prepare this plan. The school will invite the parent and perhaps the child, too, to a meeting to discuss the proposed plan.

The school team should contact the parents of the time and date of the meeting for presentation of the IEP. You should have reasonable notice of the meeting. You also have the right to bring professionals with knowledge of your child's disability to the meeting.

After the school conducts an evaluation of your child, it may conclude that your child is not entitled to special education services. You have the right to insist on another assessment, conducted independently, called an *Individualized Educational Evaluation (IEE)*. The school must pay for this evaluation. You should provide a list of suggested evaluation providers to the school and try to get the school to use one on your list. The IEE should screen for all areas of your child's suspected disability.

If the IEE does not determine that your child needs special education services, you have a right to a hearing. At the hearing you will need to have your own expert testify that your child has a disability. You should have an attorney well versed in school law to represent you. Several federal laws guarantee the right of a child with disabilities to receive the appropriate accommodations from the school such as speech therapy, special aides, physical and psychological therapy, tests without time limits, and other benefits. State laws may also provide benefits for the special education student.

Bullying

Bullying is a typical problem for students. It is not enough to expect the child to handle the situation alone. Parents and teachers must become involved. Those students participating in the teasing and bullying must be punished. If the abuse continues, parents should file a criminal complaint with the local police. They should also demand that the school district pay for a private school for their son or daughter since the school was not able to stop the abuse.

If after attempting in vain to engage the school to solve the problem, contact the school superintendent.

Taking Action—Step-by-Step

1. If your child is being bullied, you must demand that the school deal with the bully immediately. Accept nothing less than a prompt end to all endangerment to your child. Demand nothing less than absolute protection for your child.

2. The bully's parents must be confronted by the school. The bully should be told that his behavior is wrong and forbidden. The parents must be told that their child will be suspended or expelled from the school if the behavior continues (following the guidelines of the school system).

3. Complain to the principal if the teacher does not react to your concerns. If the principal will not respond, then you must complain to the school board, and then to the district superintendent. Complain to the state superintendent of education, if necessary.

NOTE: *Hazing, which has occurred among teenagers in high school and resulted in broken bones and stitches, can be considered another form of bullying. Don't hesitate to contact the school regarding these situations.*

4. If you believe your child has a learning disability or a problem requiring special services, ask the school to evaluate your child. Many parents already know their child has a problem—such as a speech impediment, depression, mental or emotional disturbances, or the child is deaf—and may skip that step by providing their own evaluation by an expert to the school.

NOTE: *If you ask the school for an evaluation for your child, the school must provide one.*

5. If you and the school agree that the child is in need of a special service, then the school must prepare an *Individual Educational Plan* or *IEP*. Many schools are resistant to providing these services. You must be assertive. If the school does not agree that your child needs special services, then you may appeal the decision to the local school board. Consider retaining an attorney to help you through this legal maze, because an appeal requires very specific steps. You must follow them exactly or lose your right to an appeal. There are attorneys who concentrate in school law.

Letter 83: Principal; Follow-Up Letter, Screening Child for Learning Disability

Jane Johnson
77 Sunset Strip
Los Angeles, Ca. 91130
213-333-7777

June 13, 2003

Mr. Osgood Conklin
Principal
Sunshine School
12 Education St.
Los Angeles, Ca. 91130

Re: Screening of David Johnson

Dear Mr. Conklin:

Please be advised that I am the mother of a second grade student in your school, David Johnson. He has difficulty paying attention in class. His teachers have complained that he speaks out of turn and disrupts the class.

We have noticed David's impatience and distraction at home, too. Our pediatrician recently examined David and suggests that you screen him for a learning disability such as Attention Deficit Disorder or Attention Deficit Hyperactivity Disorder.

I have spoken with his teacher, Mrs. Bradford, and with the counselor, Mr. Jackson, about this need. To date, I have received no response. I am now writing to you.

Please arrange this screening as soon as possible. We want to place David in the appropriate education program for the fall, if it is determined that he has a disability requiring special education.

Thank you for your prompt attention to this matter.

Very truly yours,

Jane Johnson
Cc:file

Via Certified Mail

Letter 84: Principal; Second Letter, Need to Develop Education Plan

Jane Johnson
77 Sunset Strip
Los Angeles, Ca. 91130
213-333-7777

July 1, 2003

Mr. Osgood Conklin
Principal
Sunshine School
12 Education St.
Los Angeles, Ca. 91130

Re: Screening of David Johnson

Dear Mr. Conklin:

On June 13, I sent you a request to conduct a screening of our son, David Johnson, for Attention Deficit Disorder (ADD) or Attention Deficit Hyperactivity Disorder (ADHD). We have not had any response.

Please be advised that we have obtained a screening at The University of Chicago for our son. Enclosed please find a letter from our expert, Dr. Rose Beck. She has diagnosed David with ADHD.

We want to schedule a meeting with you within the next week to arrange for the preparation of an Individualized Education Plan (IEP) for our son. This should be in place before the start of the fall semester.

Sincerely yours,

Jane Johnson
Cc:enc:file

Letter 85: Principal;
Third Letter, Child's Right to IEE

Jane Johnson
77 Sunset Strip
Los Angeles, Ca. 91130
213-333-7777

July10, 2003

Mr. Osgood Conklin
Principal
Sunshine School
12 Education St.
Los Angeles, Ca. 91130

Re: Screening of David Johnson

Dear Mr. Conklin:

On June 13 and July 1, I wrote to you to request that a screening and an Individualized Educational Plan be prepared for my son, David Johnson. We have not heard from you.

We have provided you with a copy of the report from our expert, Dr. Rose Beck, an educational psychologist at The University of Chicago.

Now we are exercising our right to have an Individualized Educational Evaluation (IEE) at your expense. We want another expert in the field of Attention Deficit Hyperactivity Disorder (ADHD) to evaluate our son. We are enclosing a list of three suggested experts from local universities. Any one of these experts is acceptable.

Please contact me by July 15th to arrange for the IEE.

Unless we hear from the school, we assume that we must take legal
action to preserve our rights.

Sincerely yours,

Jane Johnson
Cc:enc:file

Letter 86: Principal; Bullying of Child

Lawrence Reed
14 Exeter Lane
Boston, MA 33333
222-343-5656

May 31, 2003

Ms. Sarah Ambrose
Principal
Longfellow Elementary School
9009 Poets Lane
Boston, Ma. 33333

Re: Betty Reed

Dear Ms. Ambrose:

I am writing to you concerning the ongoing bullying of my daughter, Betty, occurring in your classrooms. The problem has worsened since our parent/teacher conference in April.

My daughter comes home in tears nearly every day. She reports that the children in the 6th grade class tease her unmercifully. They call her names and pinch and scratch her. At recess she has been cornered and kicked by a group of girls. These girls also call her obscene names and yell other insults at her. The playground monitor has seen this abuse, but has refused to get involved.

Something must be done to make this teasing and bullying stop. I am demanding that the school act immediately. You, as the supervisor of these children, need to address this problem. The school psychologist and other professionals need to become involved at once.This is a very serious situation. Please call me to discuss the solution to this problem.

Sincerely yours,

Lawrence Reed
Cc:file

Letter 87: Principal; Second Letter, Bullying of Child

Lawrence Reed
14 Exeter Lane
Boston, MA 33333
222-343-5656

June 24, 2003

Ms. Sarah Ambrose
Principal
Longfellow Elementary School
9009 Poets Lane
Boston, MA 33333

Re: Betty Reed

Dear Ms. Ambrose:

I have not had any response from you concerning the bullying of my daughter, Betty. Another school year has come to an end without any response from the school.

You are required to make a reasonable effort to resolve and accommodate my daughter's needs. First and foremost, you need to instruct the students involved in the bullying, their parents, and their teachers that this is not acceptable behavior. It violates the school code and state law. The behavior is cruelly directed towards a defenseless little girl for no discernible reason.

It is not adequate for the teachers to direct the children to "work it out." My child is physically and emotionally harmed by this behavior. She cannot learn in an environment where such cruelty exists.

We expect you to remedy this problem before the start of the school year in August. This should include warning the children and their parents of the consequences if the bullying continues. The school code mandates suspension and expulsion of these students.

Legal action will ensue unless you accept your responsibilities to my child. She is entitled to a school where she can learn free of harm. If you cannot provide this environment, then you should pay for us to send her to a school that can.

Very truly yours,

Lawrence Reed
Cc:file

Letter 88: Superintendent of Schools; Follow-Up Letter, Bullying of Child

Lawrence Reed
14 Exeter Lane
Boston, Ma. 33333
222-343-5656

July 1, 2003

Superintendent District 3 Schools
Dr. Nancy Foote
120 W. Highway 11
Boston, Ma. 33333

Re: Betty Reed

Dear Dr. Foote:

I am writing to you in a final effort to resolve the bad bullying situation that exists at my daughter's school, Longfellow Elementary. Previous attempts to rectify the situation have been fruitless. The teachers, the school psychologist, and the principal have not helped at all. Copies of my letters to the school principal have been ignored. (Copies of some of those letters are included here.)

I have a telephone log of my conversations with the school officials, including teachers, principal, counselors, social workers and psychologist. Nothing has helped.

Outside of school, I have talked with the parents of the children who have been bullying my daughter. They denied that their children were involved. I have watched the children at recess and during school hours. I have seen these children abusing my daughter both verbally and physically. Betty will tell you the names of the attackers, but no one at the school seems to care.

This situation cannot be allowed to persist. I am asking you to take charge of this problem immediately. Please call me to discuss this matter.

Very truly yours,

Lawrence Reed
Cc:enc:file

8 Travel

Travel has become more difficult in recent years due to changing security measures. There are many rules to follow when traveling, especially by air. Check the Federal Aviation Administration website at **www.faa.gov** and the Homeland Security website at **www.homelandsecurity.com**, in addition to your airline website, for current information.

PUBLISHER'S NOTE: *In addition to the information contained in this book, Sphinx Publishing has another title available,* Traveler's Rights: Your Legal Guide to Fair Treatment and Full Value, *to assist you with travel related concerns.* Traveler's Rights *provides an in-depth look at issues regarding air travel, car rental, lodging, cruises, tours, agents, discrimination, and much more. An appendix is devoted to* Effective Complaint Letters, *as well as* Supplements *containing nearly every airline, car rental, hotel/motel, and cruise line contact information. Complete with laws, regulations, and travel tips,* Traveler's Rights *is sure to assist you in resolving your travel-related complaints.*

Damaged or Lost Luggage

Lost or damaged luggage is a frequent problem. File your claim immediately when you reach your destination. Make sure your luggage is labeled both inside and outside with your name, address, and telephone number at home and at your destination. If your luggage is lost, but you are on vacation out of town, the airline will not be able to reach you.

The federal Transportation Security Agency (TSA) is an office of the Department of Transportation. Its employees are responsible for screening passengers and their luggage at the airports and elsewhere. The agency recommends that you travel with unlocked luggage, since it must be easily opened for security reasons. The TSA has its own claim form for missing or damaged items. It is called *SF95* and is available for download at the Transportation Security Administration website at **www.tsa.gov**. The telephone number for the TSA Contact Center is toll-free at 866-289-9673.

Be sure to get the names of the TSA employees at the airport to whom you reported your problem. Get a written description of the problem and any information you can from the TSA and your airline. Take a picture of the damage when you get to your destination. Get written estimates of repairs and/or replacements.

Passengers with Disabilities

The *Americans with Disabilities Act (ADA)* requires airline and security agencies to accommodate the needs of passengers with disabilities. The TSA (Transportation Security Administration) has advice for passengers with disabilities on its website at **www.tsa.gov/public**. If you encounter any problems with TSA employees, file a complaint in writing by sending the details of your flight— number, airport, date, time of incident, and the name of the employee to:

Transportation Security Administration
Director Office of Civil Rights
400 Seventh ST. SW
TSA-6
Washington, DC 20590-0001
Attn: External Programs Division

diabetics

If it is medically necessary for you to bring syringes on an airplane, bring a copy of your prescription, a note from your doctor, and the box with the label attached from your prescription with you in your carry on luggage. Carry the needles and the syringes with you, too. There should not be a problem.

Travel Agents

The American Society of Travel Agents (ASTA) is a national professional organization of travel agents that has a consumer affairs department. The email address is **consumeraffairs@astahg.com**. The telephone number is 703-739-2782; FAX: 703-684-8319.

The travel agency or agent must be a member of the organization in order for you to file a complaint. There is a voluntary mediation process. ASTA cannot go to court or require an agent to reimburse you.

The complaint must be travel-related and less than six months old. You must have contacted the company first to allow it to fix the problem. If you file a complaint, it must be in writing; include copies of your receipts, payments, and other necessary information. The complaint must be filed in duplicate. The Better Business Bureau in your town, the police fraud division, or your state attorney general may also be of service. You may also be able to pursue your claim in small claims court.

If the agency is bankrupt, all you can do is file a proof of claim as a creditor with the bankruptcy court. However, the chances of your recovery of funds in bankruptcy court in this type of case are very slim.

Bumped Airline Passengers

You arrive at the airport for your flight and there is not enough room for everyone with a ticket. You are bumped from your flight and told to catch the next one to your destination. What are your rights?

The U.S. Department of Transportation administered Rule 240 governing the rights of bumped passengers. Each airline is allowed to make its own written version of this rule. The rule explains what the airline will do in case a flight is delayed or canceled. You may receive a free ticket for another flight, cash, or your money may be refunded.

Hotels and Other Public Places

The *Americans With Disabilities Act* requires most public places to provide handicapped access. Some hotel frequent stay clubs have a special number to call for problems (check the back of your card).

If a letter does not bring results, then a complaint to the Office of Civil Rights and the local human rights agency should get some action. There are also handicapped advocacy groups in most major cities.

Trains

If you have trouble on the train, ask the conductor for help. The conductor is *in charge* of the passengers. The conductor may assist you in finding a handicapped seat.

Amtrak provides discounts for disabled travelers upon presentation of proof of disability such as a doctor's letter. Contact Amtrak for more information. The Amtrak website is **www.amtrak.com**. You can call 800-USA-RAIL for additional assistance.

If you booked your train trip through a travel agent, then you may wish to complain to the travel agent. If that is not successful, then you could complain to the professional travel association to which your agent belongs, if you believe your agent was at fault.

Handicapped passengers must be accommodated under the federal disability law. The washroom and aisles should be accessible. There should be wheelchair-friendly ramps to and from the trains and train station. If the disabled traveler's needs are not met, file a complaint with:

U.S. Department of Transportation
Departmental Office of Civil Rights
Office of the Secretary
400 Seventh Street, S.W., Room 10215
Washington, D.C. 20590
www.dot.gov/accessibility/complaint.html

Taxicabs

Most cities have taxicab services. A department of consumer services or a taxi commission usually regulates the taxis. This information should be posted inside the cab in plain view. If you have a complaint, start by contacting the city where the cab ride occurred. Complain to the tourist authority. Be sure to get the number of the cab and the name of the cab driver if there is any problem.

Car Rental

The car rental business is very competitive. If the car you reserved is not available, then you should ask to speak to the onsite manager at the car rental counter. After speaking with the manager, if you are not satisfied, complain to the customer service department at corporate headquarters. The next step would be to complain right to the top—the Chief Executive Officer of the company.

Many car rental agencies are franchisees. These are independent businesses that buy the rights to operate a car rental agency under the corporate name. The corporation may not have as much control over franchise operators as over its own sites. The corporation may operate its own agencies directly. You will probably have better luck obtaining satisfaction from a corporate site.

If the corporation receives too many complaints about franchise operators, it could force the franchisee to sell its operations back to the corporation. Car rental companies do not want dissatisfied customers.

Remember that most people with standard car insurance do not need to buy the extra coverage at the rental counter. Check with your insurance agent before you travel to confirm that you are covered while driving a rental car. Take your car insurance card with you when you travel.

Certain credit cards also offer car insurance coverage for rental cars. Call your credit card company and ask for the current information about extra benefits available to you.

Letter 89: Airline; Lost Luggage

Ann Passenger
3 Middle America Lane
Dayton, OH 33333
222-222-2222

May 6, 2003

United States Airlines
Lost Baggage Department
Dallas, TX 02344

Re: Lost Baggage Claim #818909

Dear Sir or Madam:

Please be advised that I was a passenger on Flight 117 from Dayton, Ohio to Chicago, Illinois (O'Hare) on April 30, 2003. My luggage was lost on this direct flight. After more than five days, you have not found my luggage.

Enclosed please find my list with receipts of items I was authorized to purchase by your ground agent, Mr. Lennox. As you can see, the list includes necessary things such as underwear, clothing, and toiletries. The total is $347.76. Please send a refund in this amount to my address listed at the top of this letter.

Please send me a claim form for the lost luggage. I would prefer to have my luggage returned to me.

Very truly yours,

Ann Passenger
Cc:enc:file

Letter 90: Department of Transportation; Repair Luggage

Bill Passenger
44 Your Town Rd.
New York, NY 12345
123-455-6666

June 6, 2003

U.S. Department of Transportation
Transportation Security Administration
Claims Office
TSA Headquarters, West Bldg., 8th Floor
601 S. 12th St. (TSA-2)
Arlington, VA 22202-4220

Re: Damaged Luggage

Dear Sir or Madam:

Please be advised that your inspector broke the lock on my luggage on May 25, 2003 at the airport in Palm Springs, California. The lock was open and did not need to be touched by anyone in order to view the contents of the suitcase. In the process of trying to open the lock, the fabric of the suitcase was ripped. The lock was broken.

Enclosed please find a note from your inspector stating that the luggage was examined and the damage caused by this inspection.

Also enclosed please find a copy of the repair estimate I received from the luggage shop where I purchased the suitcase earlier this year. As you can see, the luggage repairs are not recommended because it is doubtful that the damage can be fixed. The replacement cost for a suitcase is also noted on the estimate: $400.00.

I expect to receive reimbursement for the full amount of my loss within 14 business days. My claim form is enclosed.

Very truly yours,

Bill Passenger
Cc:enc:file

Letter 91: Department of Transportation; Stolen Item

Fred Flyer
1903 Kitty Hawk Drive
Charlotte, S.C. 45023
222-222-2222

April 4, 2003

U.S. Department of Transportation
Transportation Security Administration
Claims Office
TSA Headquarters, West Bldg., 8th Floor
601 S. 12th St. (TSA-2)
Arlington, VA 22202-4220

Re: Stolen Camera

Dear Sir or Madam:

On April 2, 2003, I flew from St. Louis to Charlotte on Rapid Transfer Airlines, Flight 12. I checked my luggage with a skycap.

When I retrieved my luggage in Charlotte, my digital camera was missing from my bag.

I reported the loss of the item in Charlotte to the airline and the TSA office. Copies of the reports are enclosed. I am also enclosing a TSA Claim Form for Missing or Damaged Items (SF95) that I downloaded from your website. A copy of my receipt for the purchase of this camera is enclosed. I had just purchased this camera for my trip.

Please remit a check to me within 14 business days.

Very truly yours,

Fred Flyer
Cc:enc:file

Letter 92: Department of Transportation; Failure to Accommodate Passenger with Disability

Caroline Smith
9214 Mulberry St.
Anytown, PA 74439
888-909-3654

February 2, 2003

U.S. Department of Transportation
Aviation Consumer Protection Division
Attn: C-75-D
400 7th St., S.W.
Washington, D.C. 20590

Re: Failure to Accommodate
Passenger with Disability

Dear Sir or Madam:

Please be advised that I am writing to register my complaint about my treatment on Pegasus Airlines, Flight # 2222, from Chicago to Los Angeles on June 1, 2003.

I am a passenger with a disability and I need a wheelchair to move more than a very short distance. There was no pre-boarding announcement allowing passengers who need more time to board first.

The gate attendant, Rose Washington, told me that the airline does not permit handicapped passengers to board first. I was also told I would have to walk to the gate. Finally, she told me that I could not bring my collapsible wheelchair onboard. This treatment violates the Americans with Disabilities Act.

Please respond at your earliest convenience.

Very truly yours,

Caroline Smith
Cc:file

Letter 93: Department of Transportation; Screening Discrimination

Barbara Oak
89 Monterey Dr.
San Diego, Ca. 03810
777-062-4588

July 8, 2003

Department of Transportation
Director of Civil Rights
Transportation Security Administration
400 Seventh St. S.W., TSA-6
Washington, D.C. 20590-0001
Attn: External Programs Division

Re: Passenger Screening
Discrimination

Dear Director:

I am a diabetic passenger who needs to carry my insulin syringes and needles with me when traveling. On July 6, 2003, I was flying from San Diego to Palm Springs, California. As I went through the passenger screening area, my bag containing the medication was searched and I was detained.

Although I showed the screener, John Jones, and his supervisor, Mary Bureaucrat, a letter from my doctor stating that he prescribed the medication and a pharmacy label with my name and the medication on it, your employees confiscated the needles and medication. They told me that this was not permitted on the airplane. I fly frequently with this medication and have never had a problem.

The medication had to be replaced immediately upon my arrival in Palm Springs, at a great inconvenience and cost to me. A copy of the bill for these prescription items is enclosed. My insulated carrier was also confiscated. The receipt for another one is also enclosed.

You discriminated against me as a person with a disability: diabetes. I am concerned that this wrongful conduct will continue unless you instruct your employees to follow your own guidelines that allow labeled medication, including needles. You should also instruct the screeners to use common sense. Their conduct was outrageous.

I expect a response, an apology, and a refund check for the receipts that I have included.

Very truly yours,

Barbara Oak
Cc:enc:file

Letter 94: Trade Organization; Travel Agency Theft

Rebecca Chase
Apt. 47
300 S. Thomas St.
Reseda, Ca. 91339
818-609-0025

March 13, 2003

American Society of Travel Agents
Consumer Affairs Department
1101 King St., Suite 200
Alexandria, VA 22314

Re: Travel Agency Theft

Dear Sir or Madam:

I am writing to complain about a dishonest travel agency, Fast Flight Company, a member of your group. On June 5, 2003, I paid cash for our honeymoon trip to Hawaii. A copy of my receipt for $3500.00 is enclosed. This amount paid for five nights in Hawaii at the Surf Hotel in Maui and round-trip airfare for two, coach class, on Honeymooner Airlines.

The travel agency manager told me that the computer was down and that he could not print out our tickets and vouchers. He did provide a brochure listing our honeymoon package. I returned the next day for our tickets and vouchers as the manager asked. Imagine my shock when the doors were locked and a sign on the door said Out of Business.

Our local newspaper reported that many other people paid for vacations that were not provided by this travel agency. We were forced to spend our honeymoon in Los Angeles, because we could not afford to pay for a Hawaii honeymoon again.

I am looking to you for compensation because this agency has dis-
appeared. The owner has left town according to the police and
newspaper reports. I have no other recourse. A copy of my receipt
and the brochure with the promised honeymoon is enclosed.

Thank you,

Rebecca Chase
Cc:enc:file

Letter 95: Airlines; Bumped Passenger

Bill Griswold
26 Sperry St.
Charleston, W.Va. 10045
888-626-4876

February 11, 2003

Pegasus Airlines
Customer Relations
P.O. Box 12
Dayton, Ohio 24850

Re: Bumped Passenger Complaint

Dear Sir or Ms.:

On January 2, 2003, I was a confirmed, ticketed passenger with a boarding pass for Flight #1800 from Palm Springs, Ca. to Charleston, W. Va. I arrived at the departure gate one hour prior to check-in where I was the first in line. I was bumped from the flight. I did not volunteer to lose my seat.

You rescheduled my flight for later in the day. The change in schedule caused me to arrive at my destination more than three hours later than scheduled. I should have received $400.00 in compensation, rather than the $300.00 you provided. The lower figure is double the face value of the ticket, but I should have received the greater sum of $400.00.

According to Rule 245, I should not have been bumped in the first place. I am seeking compensation for this violation of federal law of the Department of Transportation. Under this law, passengers should be bumped according to "first come, first served."

Please contact me to resolve this matter. I travel on your airline frequently. Please do not make me reconsider my future travel choices. Copies of my tickets for both the bumped and subsequent flights, boarding passes, with a copy of the check I received are enclosed.

Thank you,

Bill Griswold
Cc:enc:file

Letter 96: Hotel; Quoted Reservation

Anne Seth
83 Cross Court
Boston, MA 21377
515-293-1234

July 8, 2003

Premiere Hotels, Inc.
Customer Service Manager
77 Sunset Blvd.
Los Angeles, Ca.91387

Re: Quoted Reservation

Dear Sir or Madam:

On June 1, 2003, I made reservations for two double rooms at your hotel on the Internet through your website. The price quoted for each room was $125.00 per night. A copy of my confirmation with reference number is enclosed.

Imagine my surprise when my family checked in and was charged $300.00 per night/per room. I tried to show the reservations manager my confirmation information, but was told that such a low price would never be promised, despite the fact that the confirmation number was given by your corporate website.

We were in Los Angeles to attend a family member's wedding at the hotel. We paid the inflated prices under protest. A copy of the inflated bill is enclosed. Please refund the difference between the promised rate and the rate we were forced to pay.

Please honor the price you originally promised. I have always had good service at your hotels. I am a member of your Happy Hotels club. It would be unfortunate if I had to transfer my loyalty to another hotel group because of this incident.

Very truly yours,

Anne Seth
Cc:enc:file

Letter 97: Hotel; Handicapped Access

Michael Brown
90 Westminster Dr.
Spokane, WA 23245
909-256-4107

March 19, 2003

Manager
Very Fancy Hotel
700 N. Michigan Ave.
Chicago, IL 60610

Re: Handicapped Access

Dear Sir or Madam:

I had a reservation to stay at your hotel the evenings of March 11 and 12. I made my reservation through your hotel's 800 service. At that time, I informed the customer service representative that I had a disability and required a wheelchair. I asked if your hotel is fully accessible at least three times before I made the reservation. I was assured that it was. My confirmation number is enclosed.

When I arrived at your hotel to check in after a long and tiring flight, I could not even get into the lobby because of a flight of stairs. I asked the doorman if there was another entrance. He denied that there was any other way into the hotel for wheelchair guests. I asked the doorman to please get the manager, but he refused.

At this point I decided to change to an accessible hotel. I used my cell phone to call for a handicapped accessible cab. The driver recommended a few hotels where he had taken passengers in the past. I was able to find an accessible hotel after a long delay.

There is no excuse for your insensitivity to my plight. It is a violation of both local and federal law to deny people with disabilities access to your facility. Please contact me to discuss this matter.

Very truly yours,

Michael Brown
Cc:file

Letter 98: Hotel; Misrepresentation of Facility

Jane Traveler
18 University Place
Memphis, TN 80956
555-555-1212

April 15, 2003

Manager
Family Friendly Hotel
900 S. Office Park
Baltimore, MD 40933

Re: Misrepresentation of Facility

Dear Manager:

On February 5, I booked a spring trip for my family to your Orlando, Florida resort. I booked the trip online at your website and confirmed with your reservations office for a March 23-30 stay. I informed your agent that my two children were ages 4 and 6. On your website, I noted under "special needs requests" that I wanted a nice hotel that was child friendly.

I was shocked to check in on the morning of March 23 to learn that you had rented most of the hotel to college students who were packed in four or more to each single room. They were loud, obnoxious, and drunken most of the time we encountered them. The college kids played music at ear-splitting volume by the pool. They screamed at each other and used profane language in the presence of young children. Some shameless couples engaged in the type of sexual activity that polite people confine to their bedrooms. The manager refused to intervene.

We wanted to leave the hotel, but could not find reservations available elsewhere in the town. This was spring break and all rooms were taken. Your website has enticing pictures of the pool with the phrase "family friendly" written across it. Our experience was anything but suitable for a family with young children.

Please contact me so that we can discuss a solution to this problem. I believe that a fair resolution is to refund one-half of the charges for our hotel room. We were deprived of using the facilities, except to bathe and to sleep, because of the rowdy behavior of other guests. We stayed away as much as possible. A copy of the bill is enclosed.

Very truly yours,

Jane Traveler
Cc:enc:file

Letter 99: Railroad; Unsatisfactry Accommodations

Ron Railfan
863 Robin Circle
Hoboken, N.J. 12489
855-963-2087

June 2, 2003

Iron Horse Railroad
Manager of Customer Relations
P.O. Box 12
Horseshoe Pass, WY 12090

Re: Unsatisfactory Accommodations

Dear Sir or Ms.:

On May 30, 2003, I was a passenger on Train #64 traveling from Detroit to Chicago. The rail car with my assigned seat was very dirty. A dining car was supposed to be operating during the trip, offering hot food and snacks. The dining car was closed. An employee did have some boxes of candy, a few bags of pretzels, and some cans of warm soda pop for sale. This was clearly inadequate for the hundreds of passengers.

The poor service is inexcusable. I deserve a refund of a portion of my fare for the terrible conditions on this trip. A copy of my ticket is enclosed.

Very truly yours,

Ron Railfan
Cc:enc:file

Letter 100: Department of Consumer Services; Inflated Taxi Charges

Joanne Jones
103 Dobbs St.
Smalltown, U.S.A.
555-555-5555

June 5, 2003

Department of Consumer Services
Richard J. Daley Center
50 West Washington
Room 208
Chicago, Illinois 60602

Re: Inflated Charges

Dear Sir or Madam:

On May 28, I was a passenger in Cab # 2200 with driver Don Cantdrive. He took advantage of my unfamiliarity with your city. What should have been a $6.00 cab ride from the Trendy Hotel to Navy Pier, cost $35.00.

The driver also drove too fast and in a reckless manner.

Please investigate.

Very truly yours,

Joanne Jones
Cc:file

Letter 101: Car Rental Company; Breach of Contract

Car Renter
38 Western Ave.
Portland, OR 84800
502-999-8888

March 26, 2003

Manager
Friendly Automobile Rental
Western Airport
Seaside, CA 91022

Re: Breach of Contract

Dear Sir or Ms.:

On February 1, I rented a minivan through your website for a family vacation March 15-20. I need this particular vehicle to accommodate my family of seven. I charged the rental to my Visa card.

We arrived at your counter at the appointed time. Your facility did not have any minivans and did not expect to have one returned in time for us to use it. You did not have a station wagon or other vehicle suitable for my family. We had to squeeze into a large luxury car that was entirely unsuitable for young children. There was not enough room for our luggage. We had to hire a taxi to deliver the luggage to our hotel.

I believe that you should reimburse us for the taxi service for our luggage and reduce the rental rate considerably. We were at your mercy due to the demand for cars for spring vacation.

Very truly yours,

Car Renter
Cc:enc:file

State Attorneys General

Each state has a chief legal officer known as an attorney general. This lawyer is responsible for overseeing the enforcement of the laws of the state. Local prosecutors enforce the laws unless there is a conflict of interest, then the attorney general of the state may appear in court instead of the local prosecutor.

The attorney general of the state usually monitors charities and non-profit trusts to make sure that they are not fleecing donors or using charitable funds for their own purposes.

The attorney general is a powerful *consumer advocate*. The more active state officers have excellent consumer information in areas such as nursing homes, elder rights, identity theft, and Internet fraud. Each state has different laws. Activities of the attorney general may vary by state.

ALABAMA
State House
11 S. Union St.
Montgomery, AL 36130
334-242-7300
www.ago.state.al.us

ALASKA
P.O. Box 110300
Diamond Courthouse
Juneau, AK 99811-0300
907-465-3600
www.law.state.ak.us

ARIZONA
1275 W. Washington St.
Phoenix. AZ 85007
602-542-4266
www.attorneygeneral.state.az.us

ARKANSAS
200 Tower Bldg.
323 Center St.
Little Rock, AR 72201-2610
800-482-8982
www.ag.state.ar.us

CALIFORNIA
1300 I St.
Suite 1740
Sacramento, CA 95814
916-445-9555
http://caag.state.ca.us

COLORADO
Dept. of Law
1525 Sherman St.
Denver, CO 80203
303-866-4500
www.ago.state.co.us

CONNECTICUT
55 Elm St.
Hartford, CT 06141-0120
860-808-5318
www.cslib.org/attygenl/

DELAWARE
Carvel State Office Bldg.
820 N. French St.
Wilmington, DE 19801
302-577-8338
www.state.de.us/attgen

DISTRICT OF COLUMBIA
441 4th St. NW
Washington, DC 20001
202-724-1305
http://occ.dc.gov

FLORIDA
The Capitol
PL 101
Tallahassee, FL 32399-1050
850-487-1963
http://myfloridalegal.com/

GEORGIA
40 Capitol Sq., SW
Atlanta, GA 30334-1300
404-656-3300
http://ganet.org/ago

HAWAII
425 Queen St.
Honolulu, HI 96813
808-586-1500
www.state.hi.us/ag/index.html

IDAHO
Statehouse
Boise, ID 83720-1000
208-334-2400
www2.state.id.us/ag/

ILLINOIS
James R. Thompson Ctr.
100 W. Randolph St.
Chicago, IL 60601
312-814-3000
www.ag.state.il.us

INDIANA
Indiana Government Center South
5th Floor
402 W. Washington St.
Indianapolis, IN 46204
317-232-6201
www.in.gov/attorneygeneral/

IOWA
Hoover State Office Bldg.
1305 E. Walnut
Des Moines, IA 50319
515-281-5164
www.IowaAttorneyGeneral.org

KANSAS
120 S.W. 10th Ave.
2nd Fl.
Topeka, KS 66612-1597
785-296-2215
www.ink.org/public/ksag

KENTUCKY
State Capitol
Rm. 116
Frankfort, KY 40601
502-696-5300
www.law.state.ky.us

LOUISIANA
Dept. of Justice
P.O. Box 94095
Baton Rouge, LA 70804-4095
225-342-7013
www.ag.state.la.us/

MAINE
State House Station 6
Augusta, ME 04333
207-626-8800
www.state.me.us/ag

MARYLAND
200 St. Paul Place
Baltimore, MD 21202-2202
410-576-6300
www.oag.state.md.us

MASSACHUSETTS
1 Ashburton Pl.
Boston, MA 02108-1698
617-727-2200
www.ago.state.ma.us

MICHIGAN
P.O. Box 30212
525 W. Ottawa St.
Lansing, MI 48909-0212
517-373-1110
www.ag.state.mi.us

MINNESOTA
State Capitol
Suite 102
St. Paul, MN 55155
651-296-3353
www.ag.state.mn.us

MISSISSIPPI
Dept. of Justice
P.O. Box 220
Jackson, MS 39205-0220
601-359-3680
www.ago.state.ms.us

MISSOURI
Supreme Ct. Bldg.
207 W. High St.
Jefferson City, MO 65101
573-751-3321
www.ago.state.mo.us

MONTANA
Justice Bldg.
215 N. Sanders
Helena, MT 59620-1401
406-444-2026
http://doj.state.mt.us/

NEBRASKA
State Capitol
P.O. Box 98920
Lincoln, NE 68509-8920
402-471-2682
www.nol.org/home/ago

NEVADA
Old Supreme Ct. Bldg.,
100 N. Carson St.
Carson City, NV 89701
775-684-1100
http://ag.state.nv.us/

NEW HAMPSHIRE
State House Annex
25 Capitol St.
Concord, NH 03301-6397
603-271-3658

NEW JERSEY
Richard J. Hughes Justice Complex
25 Market St.
CN 080
Trenton, NJ 08625
609-292-8740
www.state.nj.us/lps/

NEW MEXICO
P.O. Drawer 1508
Santa Fe, NM 87504-1508
505-827-6000
www.ago.state.nm.us

NEW YORK
Dept. of Law
The Capitol
2nd Floor
Albany, NY 12224
518-474-7330
www.oag.state.ny.us

NORTH CAROLINA
919-716-6400
Dept. of Justice
P.O.Box 629
Raleigh, NC 27602-0629
919-716-6400
www.jus.state.nc.us

NORTH DAKOTA
State Capitol
600 E. Boulevard Ave.
Bismarck, ND 58505-0040
701-328-2210
www.ag.state.nd.us

OHIO
State Office Tower
30 E. Broad St.
Columbus, OH 43266-0410
614-466-4320
www.ag.state.oh.us

OKLAHOMA
State Capitol, Rm. 112
2300 N. Lincoln Blvd.
Oklahoma City, OK 73105
405-521-3921
www.oag.state.ok.us

OREGON
Justice Bldg.
1162 Court St., NE
Salem, OR 97301
503-378-4732
www.doj.state.or.us

PENNSYLVANIA
Strawberry Square
Harrisburg, PA 17120
717-787-3391
www.attorneygeneral.gov

PUERTO RICO
P.O.Box 9020192
San Juan, PR 00902-0192
787-721 7700
www.justicia.gobierno.pr

RHODE ISLAND
150 S. Main St.
Providence, RI 02903
401-274-4400
www.riag.state.ri.us

SOUTH CAROLINA
Rembert C. Dennis Office Bldg.
P.O.Box 11549
Columbia, SC 29211-1549
803-734-4399
www.scattorneygeneral.org

SOUTH DAKOTA
500 E. Capitol
Pierre, SD 57501-5070
605-773-3215
www.state.sd.us/attorney/attorney.html

TENNESSEE
500 Charlotte Ave.
Nashville, TN 37243
615-741-5860
www.attorneygeneral.state.tn.us

TEXAS
Capitol Station
P.O.Box 12548
Austin, TX 78711-2548
512-463-2100
www.oag.state.tx.us

UTAH
State Capitol, Rm. 236
Salt Lake City, UT 84114-0810
801-538-9600
http://attorneygeneral.utah.gov/

VERMONT
109 State St.
Montpelier, VT 05609-1001
802-828-3173
www.state.vt.us/atg

VIRGINIA
900 E. Main St.
Richmond, VA 23219
804-786-2071
www.oag.state.va.us

WASHINGTON
P.O.Box 40100
1125 Washington St., SE
Olympia, WA 98504-0100
360-753-6200
www.wa.gov/ago

WEST VIRGINIA
State Capitol
1900 Kanawha Blvd., E.
Charleston, WV 25305
304-558-2021
www.state.wv.us/wvag

WISCONSIN
State Capitol, Ste. 114 E.
P.O.Box 7857
Madison, WI 53707-7857
608-266-1221
www.doj.state.wi.us

WYOMING
State Capitol Bldg.
Cheyenne, WY 82002
307-777-7841
http://attorneygeneral.state.wy.us

State Securities Administrators

Each state has its own laws and regulations for securities brokers and for all types of securities, including stocks, mutual funds, commodities, real estate offerings, uninsured investment products sold by banks and others. The officials and agencies listed below enforce these laws and regulations. Many of these offices can provide you with information to help you make informed investment decisions.

State securities agencies are also responsible for preventing fraud and abuse in the sale of all but the largest securities offerings. If you have a question or complaint about an investment you have made or are about to make, call the company or bank involved. If your complaint or question is not resolved, call the appropriate state securities agency.

ALABAMA
Director
Securities Commission
770 Washington Ave.
Suite 570
Montgomery, AL 36130-4700
334-242-2984
In AL: 800-222-1253
Fax: 334-242-0240
Email: alseccom@dsmd.dsmd.state.al.us
www.state.al

ALASKA

Senior Examiner
Department of Commerce and Economic Development
PO Box 110807
150 Third St., Room 217
Juneau, AK 99801
907-465-2521
Fax: 907-465-2549
www.dced.state.ak.us/bsc/bsc.htm

ARIZONA

Director of Securities
Arizona Corporation Commission
Securities Division
1300 West Washington
3rd Floor
Phoenix, AZ 85040
602-542-4242
Fax: 602-594-7470
Email: accsec@ccsd.cc.state.az.us
www.ccsd.cc.state.az.us

ARKANSAS

Securities Division
Heritage West Building
201 East Markham, 3rd Floor
Little Rock, AR 72201-1692
501-324-9260
800-981-4429
Fax: 501-324-9268
Email: securities@mail.state.ar.us

CALIFORNIA

California Corporations Commissioner
Department of Corporations
1515 K St., Suite 200
Sacramento, CA 95814-4052
916-445-7205
www.corp.ca.gov

COLORADO

Securities Commissioner
Colorado Division of Securities
1580 Lincoln St., Suite 420
Denver, CO 80203-1506
303-894-2320
Fax: 303-861-2126
www.dora.state.co.us/securities

CONNECTICUT

Banking Commissioner
Department of Banking
260 Constitution Plaza
Hartford, CT 06103-1800
860-240-8299
800-831-7225
Fax: 860-240-8178
www.state.ct.us/dob

DELAWARE

Securities Commissioner
Department of Justice
Division of Securities
State Office Building
820 North French Street, 5th Floor
Wilmington, DE 19801
302-577-8424
Fax: 302-577-6987
www.state.de.us/securities

DISTRICT OF COLUMBIA

Commissioner
Department of Insurance and Securities Regulation
810 First St., NW
Suite 701
Washington, DC 20002
202-727-8000
Fax: 202-535-1196
Email: disr@dcgov.org

FLORIDA

Comptroller
Division of Securities
101 East Gaines St.
Tallahassee, FL 32399-0350
850-410-9805
In FL: 800-372-3792
Fax: 850-681-2428
www.dbf.state.fl.us

GEORGIA

Division of Securities and Business Regulation
Office of the Secretary of State
802 West Tower
Two Martin Luther King, Jr. Drive
Atlanta, GA 30334
404-656-3920
888-733-7427
Fax: 404-657-8410
Email: securities@sos.state.ga.us
www.sos.state.ga.us

HAWAII

Commissioner of Securities
Department of Commerce and Consumer Affairs
Business Registration Division
1010 Richards St.
2nd Floor
Honolulu, HI 96813
808-586-2744
Fax: 808-586-2733
www.hawaii.gov

IDAHO

Bureau Chief
Securities Bureau
PO Box 83720
Boise, ID 83720-0031
208-332-8004
In ID: 888-346-3378
Fax: 208-332-8099
www.state.id.us./finance/dof.htm

ILLINOIS

Illinois Secretary of State
Securities Department
520 South Second St.
Suite 200
Springfield, IL 62701
217-782-2256
217-524-0652
In IL: 800-628-7937
www.sos.state.il.us

INDIANA

Securities Commissioner
Securities Division
Office of the Secretary of State
302 West Washington
Room E-111
Indianapolis, IN 46204
317-232-6681
In IN: 800-223-8791
Fax: 317-233-3675
www.state.in.us/sos

IOWA

Enforcement Section
Iowa Securities Bureau
Enforcement Section
340 Maple St.
Des Moines, IA 50325
515-281-4441
800-351-4665
Fax: 515-281-3059
Email: iowasec@max.state.ia.us
www.iid.state.ia.us/division/securities/default.asp

KANSAS
Commissioner
Office of the Kansas Securities Commissioner
618 South Kansas Ave.
2nd Floor
Topeka, KS 66603-3804
785-296-3307
In KS: 800-232-9580
Fax: 785-296-6872
Email: ksecom@cjnetworks.com
www.ink.org/public/ksecom

KENTUCKY
Commissioner
Department of Financial Institutions
1025 Capitol Center Dr., Suite 200
Frankfort, KY 40601-3868
502-573-3390
800-223-2579
Fax: 502-573-8787
www.dfi.state.ky.us

LOUISIANA
Deputy Commissioner of Securities
Office of Financial Institutions Securities Division
8660 United Plaza Blvd., 2nd Floor
Baton Rouge, LA 70809
225-925-4512
Fax: 225-925-4548
www.ofi.state.la.us

MAINE
Supervisor of Enforcement
Bureau of Banking
Securities Division
121 State House Station
Augusta, ME 04333-0121
207-624-8551
In ME only: 800-624-8551
Fax: 207-624-8590
www.mainesecuritiesreg.org

MARYLAND
Securities Commissioner
Office of the Attorney General
Securities
200 Saint Paul Place, 20th Floor
Baltimore, MD 21202-2020
410-576-6360
Fax: 410-576-6532
Email: securities@oag.state.md.us
www.securities.oag.state.md.us

MASSACHUSETTS
Secretary of the Commonwealth
Securities Division
One Ashburton Place
Room 1701
Boston, MA 02108
617-727-3548
In MA: 800-269-5428
Fax: 617-248-0177
www.state.ma.us/sec/sct

MICHIGAN
Office of Financial and Insurance Services
PO Box 30220
Lansing, MI 48909
517-373-0220
Fax: Fax: 517-335-4978
www.michigan.gov/cis/

MINNESOTA
Commissioner of Commerce
Department of Commerce
133 East Seventh St.
St. Paul, MN 55101
651-296-4026
In MN: 800-657-3602
Fax: 651-296-4328
www.commerce.state.mn.us

MISSISSIPPI
Assistant Secretary of State
MS Secretary of State's Office
Business Regulation and Enforcement
202 North Congress St., Suite 500
Jackson, MS 39202
601-359-1633
800-256-3494
Fax: 601-359-2663
Email: jnelson@sos.state.ms.us
www.sos.state.ms.us

MISSOURI
Commissioner of Securities
PO Box 1276
Jefferson City, MO 65102
573-751-4136
In MO: 800-721-7996
Fax: 573-526-3124
www.mose.sos.state.mo.us

MONTANA
State Auditor & Securities Commissioner
Securities Division
Office of the State Auditor
840 Helena Ave.
Helena, MT 59601
406-444-2040
In MT: 800-332-6148
Fax: 406-444-3497
www.state.mt.us/sao

NEBRASKA
Assistant Director
Department of Banking & Finance
Bureau of Securities
Suite 311, The Atrium
1200 N St.
Lincoln, NE 68509-5006
402-471-3445
www.ndbf.org

NEVADA
Chief Compliance Enforcement Investigator
Securities Division
Office of the Secretary of State
555 East Washington Ave.
Suite 5200
Las Vegas, NV 89101
702-486-2440
800-758-6440
Fax: 702-486-2452
www.sos.state.nv.us

Criminal Investigator III
Nevada Secretary of State
Securities Enforcement
1105 Terminal Way, Ste 211
Reno, NV 89502
775-688-1855
800-758-6440
Fax: 775-688-1858
www.sos.state.nv.us

NEW HAMPSHIRE
Director of Securities
Bureau of Securities Regulation
Department of State
State House, Room 204
Concord, NH 03301-4989
603-271-1463
Fax: 603-271-7933
http://webster.state.nh.us/sos/securities

NEW JERSEY
Bureau Chief
Department of Law and Public Safety
Division of Consumer Affairs, Bureau of Securities
153 Halsey Street, 6th Floor
Newark, NJ 07102
973-504-3600
Fax: 973-504-3601
www.state.nj.us/lps/ca/home.htm

NEW MEXICO

Regulation & Licensing Department
Securities Division
725 St. Michaels Drive
Santa Fe, NM 87505-7605
505-827-7140
Fax: 505-984-0617
www.rld.state.nm.us

NEW YORK

Bureau Chief
New York State Department of Law
Bureau of Investor Protection and Securities
Office of the Attorney General
120 Broadway, 23rd Floor
New York, NY 10271
212-416-8200
Fax: 212-416-8816
www.oag.state.ny.us

NORTH CAROLINA

Secretary of State
Securities Division
300 North Salisbury St.
Raleigh, NC 27603-5909
919-733-3924
800-688-4507
Fax: 919-821-0818
www.state.nc.us/secstate/

NORTH DAKOTA

North Dakota Securities Commissioner
State Capitol, 5th Floor
600 East Boulevard Avenue - Dept 414
Bismarck, ND 58505-0510
701-328-2910
In ND: 800-297-5124
Fax: 701-255-3113
Email: seccom@state.nd.us
www.state.nd.us/securities

OHIO

Commissioner
Division of Securities
77 South High St.
22nd Floor
Columbus, OH 43215
614-644-7381
800-788-1194
Fax: 614-466-3316
www.securities.state.oh.us

OKLAHOMA

Administrator
Department of Securities
First National Center
120 North Robinson, Suite 860
Oklahoma City, OK 73102
405-280-7700
Fax: 405-280-7742
Email: ods.general@oklaoss.state.ok.us
www.securities.state.ok.us

OREGON

Administrator
Division of Finance & Corporate Securities
350 Winter St., NE
Room 21
Salem, OR 97310
503-378-4387
503-378-4140
Fax: 503-947-7862
Email: dcbs.dfcsmail@state.or.us

Duty Examiner
Division of Finance and Corporate Securities
Securities Section
350 Winter St., NE, Suite 410
Salem, OR 97310
503-378-4140
503-378-4387
Fax: 503-947-7862
Email: dcbs.fcsmail@state.or.us
www.cbs.state.or.us/external/dfcs/index.html

PENNSYLVANIA
Personnel Director
Pennsylvania Securities Commission
Management Services
Eastgate Office Building 2nd Floor
1010 North 7th Street
Harrisburg, PA 17102-1410
717-783-4689
717-787-8061
In PA: 877-881-6388
Fax: 717-783-5125
www.psc.state.pa.us

PUERTO RICO
Commissioner
Securities Division
Office of the Commissioner of Financial Institutions
Fernandez Juncos Station
PO Box 11855
San Juan, PR 00910-3855
787-723-3131
Fax: 787-723-4042
www.cif.gov.pr

RHODE ISLAND
Associate Director and Superintendent of Securities
Rhode Island Department of Business Regulation
Securities Division
233 Richmond St.
Suite 232
Providence, RI 02903-4232
401-222-3048
Fax: 401-222-5629
Email: mpicciri@dbr.state.ri.us

SOUTH CAROLINA
Deputy of Securities Commissioner
Attorny Generals Office
Securities Section, Rembert C Dennis Office Building
1000 Assembly Street
Columbia, SC 29201
803-734-9916
Fax: 803-734-0032
www.lpitr.state.sc.us/code/statmast.htm

SOUTH DAKOTA
Director
Division of Securities
118 West Capitol Ave.
Pierre, SD 57501-2013
605-773-4823
Fax: 605-773-5953
www.state.sd.us/dcr/securities

TENNESSEE
Assistant Commissioner
Tennessee Department of Commerce and Insurance
Securities
Davy Crockett Tower, Suite 680
500 James Robertson Parkway
Nashville, TN 37243
615-741-2947
615-741-5900
In TN:800-863-9117
www.state.tn.us/commerce/

TEXAS
Securities Commissioner
State Securities Board
PO Box 13167
Austin, TX 78711-3167
512-305-8300
Fax: 512-305-8310
www.ssb.state.tx.us

UTAH
Director
Utah Department of Commerce
Division of Securities
160 East 300 South 2nd Floor
PO Box 146760
Salt Lake City, UT 84114-6760
801-530-6600
In UT: 800-721-7233
Fax: 801-530-6980
Email: security@br.state.ut.us
www.commerce.state.ut.us

VERMONT
Deputy Commissioner for Securities
Vermont Department of Banking, Insurance, Securities, & Health Care Administration
Securities Division
89 Main St.
Drawer 20
Montpelier, VT 05620-3101
802-828-3420
Fax: 802-828-2896
www.bishca.state.vt.us

VIRGINIA
Director
Division of Securities and Retail Franchising
State Corporation Commission
PO Box 1197
Richmond, VA 23218
804-371-9051
In VA: 800-552-7945
Fax: 804-371-9911
www.state.va.us/scc/division/srf

WASHINGTON
Administrator
Department of Financial Institutions
Securities
PO Box 9033
Olympia, WA 98507-9033
360-902-8760
Fax: 360-586-5068
www.wa.gov/dfi/securities

WEST VIRGINIA
Deputy Commissioner of Securities
Securities Division
State Auditor's Office
106 Dee Dr.
Charleston, WV 25311
304-558-2257
888-509-6567
Fax: 304-558-4211
www.wvauditor.com

WISCONSIN
Administrator
Division of Securities
Department of Financial Institutions
PO Box 1768
Madison, WI 53702-1768
608-266-3432
In WI: 800-47-CHECK
Fax: 608-256-1259
www.wdfi.org

WYOMING
Secretary of State
Securities Division
State Capitol Building
200 West 24th Street
Cheyenne, WY 82002-0020
307-777-7370
Fax: 307-777-5339
Email: securities@state.wy.us
soswy.state.wy.us

State Department of Insurance Regulators

The sale of insurance is regulated by each state. Contacting your state regulator is the next step to follow if your complaint letter has not produced a satisfactory result. Many states have websites that have online complaint forms. Following is a list of some state insurance regulators.

ALABAMA
Alabama Department of Insurance
Life and Health Division
P.O. Box 303351
Montgomery, AL 36130-3351
334-241-4141
www.alabama.gov

ALASKA
Alaska Division of Insurance
Consumer Services Section
550 W. 7th Ave.
Suite 1560
Anchorage, AK 99501
907-269-7900
In Alaska: 800-INSURAK
Fax: 907-269-7910
www.dced.state.ak.us/insurance/complaintform.htm

ARKANSAS

Arkansas Insurance Department
Consumer Services Division
Third and Cross Streets
Little Rock, AR 72201
501-371-2640
800-852-5494
Fax: 501-371-2749
www.state.ar.us/insurance/

CALIFORNIA

California Department of Insurance
Consumer Services and Market Conduct Branch
Consumer Services Division
300 S. Spring St.
South Tower
Los Angeles, Ca. 90013
800-927-HELP
www.insurance.ca.gov

COLORADO

Department of Insurance
1560 Broadway, Suite 850
Denver, CO 80202
303-894-7499
800-930-3745
Fax: 303-894-7455
www.dora.state.co.us/insurance/

DELAWARE

Department of Insurance
841 Silver Lake Blvd.
Dover, DE 19904-2465
302-739-6775
800-282-8611 (in Delaware only)
FAX: 302-739-6278
Email: consumer@deins.state.de.us
www.state.de.us/inscom/

DISTRICT OF COLUMBIA
Department of Insurance and Securities Regulation
810 First Street, NE, Suite 701
Washington, DC 20002
202-727-8000
Fax: 202-535-1196
http://disr.washingtondc.gov/main.shtm

GEORGIA
Two Martin Luther King, Jr. Drive
West Tower, Suite 704
Atlanta, Georgia 30334
404-656-2070
800-656-2298
Fax: 404-657-8542
www.gainsurance.org

HAWAII
Hawaii Insurance Division
Investigative Branch
250 S. King St.
5th Floor
Honolulu, HI 96813
808-586-2790
www.state.hi.us/dcca/ins

IDAHO
Idaho Department of Insurance
Attention: Consumer Assistance
P. O. Box 83720
Boise, ID 83720-0043
800-721-3272
www.doi.state.id.us

ILLINOIS
Illinois Department of Insurance
320 W. Washington St.
Springfield, IL 62767-0001
866-445-5364
www.ins.state.il.us

INDIANA
Indiana Department of Insurance
Consumer Services
311 W. Washington St.
Suite 300
Indianapolis, IN 46204-2767
317-232-2385
Fax: 317-232-5251
800-622-4461 (toll free in Indiana only)
www.in.gov/idoi

IOWA
Iowa Insurance Division
330 Maple St.
Des Moines, IA 50319-0065
Des Moines Area: 515-281-5705
877-955-1212
Fax: 515-281-3059
www.iid.state.ia.us

KANSAS
Kansas Insurance Department
420 SW 9th Street
Topeka, Kansas 66612-1678
800-432-2484
www.ksinsurance.org

LOUISIANA
Louisiana Department of Insurance
1702 N. 3rd Street
Baton Rouge, LA 70802
800-259-5300
www.ldi.la.gov

MAINE
Bureau of Insurance
34 State House Station
Augusta, ME 04333
800-300-5000
207-624-8475
FAX: 207-624-8599
www.MaineInsuranceReg.org

MARYLAND
Maryland Insurance Administration
525 St Paul Place
Baltimore, MD 21202-2272
410-468-2000
800-492-6116
www.mdinsurance.state.md.us

MASSACHUSETTS
Department of Insurance
One South St.
Boston, MA 02110-2208
617-521-575
www.state.ma.us/doi

MICHIGAN
Financial and Insurance Services
P.O. Box 30220
Lansing, MI 48909
877-999-6442
www.michigan.gov/cis

MINNESOTA
Minnesota Department of Commerce
85 7th Place East, Suite 500
St. Paul, MN 55101
651-297-7161
Fax: 651-296-9434
www.state.mn.us/cgi-bin/portal/mn/jsp/home.do?agency=Commerce

MISSISSIPPI
Mississippi Insurance Department
1001 Woolfolk State Office Bldg.
501 N. West St.
Jackson, MS 39201
800-562-2957
www.doi.state.ms.us

Mail complaints to:
Mississippi Insurance Department
Consumer Services Division
P.O. Box 79
Jackson, MS 39205

MISSOURI

Missouri Department of Insurance
301 West High Street
P.O. Box 690
Jefferson City, Missouri 65102
573-751-4126
www.insurance.state.mo.us

MONTANA

840 Helena Ave.
Helena, MT 59601
800-332-6148
406-444-2040
http://sao.state.mt.us/

NEBRASKA

Terminal Building
941 "O" Street, Suite 400
Lincoln, NE 68508-3639
402-471-2201
www.nol.org/home/ndoi

NEVADA

Carson City Office:
788 Fairview Drive
Suite 300
Carson City, Nevada 89701
775-687-4270
Fax: 775-687-3937
http://doi.state.nv.us/

Las Vegas Office:
2501 East Sahara Avenue
Suite 302
Las Vegas, Nevada 89104
702-486-4009
Fax: 702-486-4007

NEW HAMPSHIRE

Insurance Department
56 Old Suncook Rd.
Concord NH 03301-7317
800-852-3416
603-271-2261
Fax: 603-271-1406
www.state.nh.us/insurance

NEW JERSEY

Division of Insurance
P.O. Box 325
Trenton, NJ 08625
609-292-5360
609-292-5316
www.state.nj.us/dobi/index.shtml

NEW MEXICO

P.E.R.A. Building
1120 Paseo de Peralta
Santa Fe, NM 87504-1269
505-827-4601
Fax: 505-827-4734
www.nmprc.state.nm.us/insurance/inshm.htm

NEW YORK

New York Department of Insurance
One Commerce Plaza
Albany, NY 12257
518-474-6600
www.ins.state.ny.us

NORTH CAROLINA

North Carolina Department of Insurance
PO Box 26387
Raleigh, NC 27611
800-546-5664
919-733-2032
www.ncdoi.com

NORTH DAKOTA

North Dakota Department of Insurance
600 E Boulevard, Dept. 401
Bismarck, ND 58505-0320
800-247-0560
www.state.nd.us/ndins

OHIO

Ohio Department of Insurance
Consumer Services
2100 Stella Court
Columbus, OH 43215-1067
800-686-1526
614-644-2658
FAX 614-644-3744
www.ohioinsurance.gov

OKLAHOMA

Shepherd Mall Office:
2401 N.W. 23rd, Suite 28
Oklahoma City, OK 73152-3408
405-521-2828
800-522-0071
www.oid.state.ok.us/

Tulsa Office:
3105 E. Skelly Drive, Suite 305
Tulsa, OK 74127
918-747-7700
800-728-2906

OREGON

Oregon Insurance Division
P.O. Box 14480
Salem, OR 97309-0405
503-947-7980
Fax: 503-378-4351
www.cbs.state.or.us/external/ins

PENNSYLVANIA
REGIONAL OFFICES

Harrisburg:
Room 1321, Strawberry Square
Harristown State Office Bldg. #1
Harrisburg, PA 17120
717-787-2317
Fax: 717-787-8585

Philadelphia:
Room 1701 State Office Bldg.
1400 Spring Garden Street
Philadelphia, PA 19130
215-560-2630
Fax: 215-560-2648
www.ins.state.pa.us/ins

Pittsburgh:
Room 304 State Office Bldg.
300 Liberty Avenue
Pittsburgh, PA 15222
412-565-5020
Fax: 412-565-7648

Erie:
Room 808, Renaissance Center
10th & State Streets - PO Box 6142
Erie, PA 16512
814-871-4466
Fax: 814-871-4888

RHODE ISLAND
Department of Business Regulation
Insurance Division
223 Richmond Street
Suite 233
Providence, RI 02903-4233
401-222-2223
FAX: 401-222-5475
www.dbr.state.ri.us/insurance.html

SOUTH CAROLINA
South Carolina Department of Insurance
300 Arbor Lake Drive
Ste. 1200
Columbia, SC 29223
803-737-6160
www.doi.state.sc.us/

SOUTH DAKOTA
Department of Insurance
445 E. Capitol Ave.
Pierre, SD 57501
605-773-3563
FAX: 605-773-5360
www.state.sd.us/drr2/reg/insurance/

TENNESSEE
Department of Commerce & Insurance
Davy Crockett Tower, Suite 500
Nashville, TN 37243-0565
615-741-6007
www.state.tn.us/commerce/insurance/index.html

TEXAS
Texas Department of Insurance
333 Guadalupe
Austin, TX 78701
512-463-6169
800-578-4677
www.tdi.state.tx.us/consumer/indexc.html

UTAH
Utah Insurance Department
State Office Building, Room # 3110
Salt Lake City, Utah 84114-6901
800-439-3805
801-538-3800
Fax: 801-538-3829
www.insurance.utah.gov

VERMONT
Insurance Division
Department of Banking, Insurance, Securities
& Health Care Administration
89 Main St. Drawer 20
Montpelier, VT 05620-3101
802-828-3301
www.bishca.state.vt.us/InsurDiv/insur_index.htm

WASHINGTON
Office of Insurance
Commissioner Mike Kreidler
P.O. Box 40256
Olympia, WA 98504-0256
360-725-7080
800-562-6900
FAX: 360-586-2018
www.insurance.wa.gov/consumers/complaint.asp

WEST·VIRGINIA
West Virginia Department of Insurance
1124 Smith St.
Charleston, WV 25301
800-642-9004

WISCONSIN
Office of the Commissioner of Insurance
125 South Webster Street
Madison, Wisconsin 53702
608-266-3585, Madison
800-236-8517, statewide
FAX: Complaints: 608-264-8115
http://oci.wi.gov/oci_home.htm

WYOMING
Herschler Bldg. 3rd Fl. East
122 W. 25th St.
Cheyenne, WY 82002
307-777-7401
In Wyoming: 800-438-5768
FAX: 307-777-5895
http://insurance.state.wy.us

D State Do Not Call Information

Each state has its own rules about the Do Not Call Registry. Many states have dropped their individual registries since the federal registry opened in June, 2003. Some states have their own registries *and* their own enforcement methods. Everyone is entitled to use the federal Do Not Call Registry regardless of the state in which he or she lives. If you sign up for the federal Do Not Call Registry, you will receive full protection of this law. The federal Do Not Call law is regulated by the Federal Trade Commission (FTC). Registration is free. (It is likely that most states, after a time, will drop their individual registries and let the federal governemnt handle this issue.)

ALABAMA

Adopted FTC program.

ALASKA

Maintains own list; will not adopt FTC program as its own.
Alaskans must register separately for FTC and state lists.
To register for Alaska program online:
www.law.state.ak.us/consumer/tele_alaska.html

ARIZONA

Adopted FTC program.

ARKANSAS

Adopted FTC program and maintains own state-specific list.

To register for Arkansas program online:

www.donotcall.org

CALIFORNIA

Adopted FTC program and list as its own.

Will share names already registered on state site.

COLORADO

Adopted FTC program and maintains own state list.

To register for Colorado program online:

www.coloradonocall.com

CONNECTICUT

Adopted FTC program as its own.

Will share state names already registered with FTC.

DELAWARE

Does not have a state law. FTC registry only.

DISTRICT OF COLUMBIA

Does not have a district law. FTC registry only.

FLORIDA

Adopted FTC program.

Will continue to maintain state registry.

To register for Florida program online:

www.800helpfla.com

GEORGIA

Maintains own list; will not adopt FTC program.

Georgians must register separately for FTC and state lists.

To register for Georgia program online:

www.ganocall.com

HAWAII

Does not have a state law. FTC registry only.

IDAHO

Maintains own list; will not share with FTC.

State residents must register for FTC and state program separately.

To register for Idaho program online:

www.state.id.us/ag

ILLINOIS

Adopted FTC law and registry as its own; will share names.

Register with FTC.

INDIANA

Maintains own list; will not share with FTC.

State residents must register for FTC and state program separately.

To register for Indiana program online:

www.in.gov/attorneygeneral/telephoneprivacy

IOWA

Does not have a state law. FTC registry only.

KANSAS

Adopted FTC program and will share names from state registry.

KENTUCKY:

Adopted FTC program; will share names from state registry; and, will maintain own state registry.

To register for Kentucky program online:

www.kycallo.net

LOUISIANA

Maintains own state list.

Citizens of this state must register both with FTC and Louisiana to receive protections of both state and federal law.

To register for Louisiana program online:

www.lpsc.org/donotcall.

MAINE

Adopted FTC program as its own.

Will share names already on state list.

MARYLAND

Does not have a state law. FTC registry only.

MASSACHUSETTS

Adopted FTC program; will share names; continues to maintain state list.

To register for Massachusetts program online:

www.madonotcall.govconnect.com/Welcome.asp

*The list is published quarterly. Consumers may register by telephone at: 866-231-2255 or by regular mail at the Office of Consumer Affairs and Business Regulations, P.O. Box 1348, Boston, MA 02117.

MICHIGAN

Adopted FTC law as its own. FTC registry only.

MINNESOTA

Will share state list with FTC.

Maintains state registry.

To register for Minnesota program online:

www.165.193.128.51/dms/nocall/nocall_register_start.asp

MISSISSIPPI

Does not have state registry yet, but one is in development.

FTC registry only at this time.

MISSOURI

Will not share state list with FTC.

Residents must register with both FTC and state to receive federal and state law protection.

To register for Missouri program online:

www.ago.start.mo.us/nocalllaw.htm

MONTANA

Recently adopted FTC law and list as its own.

Register with FTC.

NEVADA

Recently adopted FTC law and list as its own.

Register with FTC.

NEW HAMPSHIRE

No state law.

Register with FTC.

NEW JERSEY

Developing state list. Register with FTC.

NEW MEXICO

Recently adopted FTC law and list as its own.

Register with FTC.

NEW YORK

Adopted FTC list as its own.

Register with FTC.

Will share names already on state list.

NORTH CAROLINA

No state law.

Register with FTC.

NORTH DAKOTA

Adopted FTC law and registry as its own.

Will share names already registered.

OHIO

No state law.

Register with FTC.

OKLAHOMA

Adopted FTC registry and will share names.

To register for Oklahoma program online:

www.oag.state.ok.us/oagweb.nsf/donotcall!openpage

OREGON

Adopted FTC registry and will share names.

More information about federal and Oregon do not call laws online at:

www.doj.state.or.us

PENNSYLVANIA

Legislation pending as of end of June, 2003 would adopt FTC list as its own.

For current information, consult the FTC or Pennsylvania law at:

www.ftc.gov/opa/2003/06/dnc/pa.htm

RHODE ISLAND

No state law.

Register with FTC.

SOUTH CAROLINA

No state law.

Register with FTC.

SOUTH DAKOTA

Adopted FTC list as state do not call list.

Register with FTC.

TENNESSEE

Will not share names on state list with FTC.

Must register with FTC.

To register for Tennessee program online:

www2.state.tn.us/tra/nocall.htm.

TEXAS

Will not share names on state list with FTC.

Must register with FTC.

To register for Texas program online:

www.texasnocall.com

UTAH

Recently enacted a do not call law.

Must register with FTC.

To register for Utah program online:

www.commerce.utah.gov/dcp/donotcall/overview.html

VERMONT

Will not share names on existing state list with FTC, but has adopted FTC registry as its own.

If you signed up on Vermont list before July 1, 2003, sign up with FTC.

VIRGINIA

No state law.

FTC registry only.

WASHINGTON

No state law.

FTC registry only.

WEST VIRGINIA

No state law.

FTC registry only.

WISCONSIN:

Will not share names on its state list.

Must register with FTC.

To register for Wisconsin program online:

http://nocall.wisconsin.gov/web/home/asp

WYOMING:

Will not share names on its state list.

Must register with FTC and with Wyoming.

State will maintain separate do not call list.

Contact Wyoming Attorney General's office for further information.

U.S. Military Consumer Services Programs

Members of the military have resources at their disposal to assist with consumer problems. The *Soldiers' and Sailors Relief Act of 1940* protects members of the military on active duty from any civil legal action taken against them. Lawsuits against them for divorce, eviction from rental property costing less than $1200 per month, and debt collections suits cannot proceed while they are on active duty.

Family Centers, located on most military installations, provide information, life skills education, and support services to military members and their families. One of the primary functions of the Family Center is to link customers with appropriate services available in the local community or through state and federal assistance programs.

Each service refers to the Family Center by a different name. If you cannot locate a Family Center, contact your respective military branch's headquarters office listed in this appendix. (The designation "DSN" preceding some of the phone numbers, refers to the military phone system and does not apply to the civilian sector.)

Access to a directory of Family Centers by service and by state is available through the *Military Family Resource Center (MFRC)* web site at **www.mfrc-dodqol.org**. If you have questions concerning other services of MFRC, visit the web site or email them at **mfrc@hq.odedodea.edu**.

U.S. Air Force
Family Matters Office
HQ US Air Force, Force Sustainment Division
HQ F/DPDF
1040 Air Force Pentagon, Room 5C238
Washington, DC 20330-1040
703-695-0242
DSN: 225-0242
Fax: 703-695-7262
DSN Fax: 225-7626
www.afcrossroads.com

U.S. Army
Community and Family Support Center
4700 King St.
Alexandria, VA 22302
703-681-7395
DSN: 761-5375
Fax: 703-681-7236
DSN Fax: 761-7236

U.S. Coast Guard
Work/Life Program
Commandant, U.S. Coast Guard
2100 Second St. SW, Room 6320
Washington, DC 20593
202-267-6263
Fax: 202-267-4798
www.uscg.mil/css/worklife/default.html

U.S. Marine Corps
Personnel Services
Programs, Personnel & Family Readiness (MRT)
3280 Russell Rd.
Quantico, VA 22134-5103
703-784-9546
DSN: 278-9501
Fax: 703-784-9816
DSN Fax: 278-9816
www.usmc-mccs.org

U.S. Navy
Family Service Center
HQ, FSC Support
NPC 660 FSC Branch
5720 Integrity Drive
Millington, TN 38085-6000
901-874-4328
DSN: 882-4328
Fax: 901-874-2785
DSN Fax: 882-2785
www.lifelines2000.org

F
Automobile Manufacturers' Customer Service Departments

Car manufacturers are very eager for your business. They are usually responsive to consumer complaints about bad experiences with dealers. If there are too many complaints, the manufacturer can cancel the dealer's contract.

Start by complaining to your zone office. This is the regional center for the automobile manufacturer. Many complaints are resolved at this level.

If you cannot receive satisfaction at this point, then complain to the manufacturer's headquarters. Contact the customer service department or consumer relations department. If that fails, then complain to the Chief Executive Officer of the company. If you have a complaint that may require legal attention, contact the general counsel's office of the manufacturer.

This appendix lists automobile manufacturers that offer complaint resolution. You must ask for a list of each company's rules before agreeing to submit your claim. For further information, see the government website at **www.pueblo.gsa.gov/crh/carman.htm.**

Car Manufacturers

If you have a problem with a car purchased from a local dealer, first try to work it out with the dealer. If the problem is not resolved, contact the manufacturer's regional or national office. Ask for the consumer affairs office. Many of these are listed in this section.

If you are still unsuccessful, consider contacting the other organizations in this section that handle consumer complaints. These programs are usually called *alternative dispute resolution programs*. Generally, there are three types: arbitration, conciliation, and mediation. All three methods of dispute resolution are different. Ask for a copy of the rules of the program before you file your case. Generally, the decisions of the arbitrators are binding and must be accepted by both the customer and the business. However, in other forms of dispute resolution, only the business is required to accept the decision. In some programs, decisions are not binding on either party.

Before contacting one of these programs, try to resolve the complaint with the company. If you still cannot resolve your problem, contact one of the third-party resolution programs. Be sure to contact your local or state consumer agency to see if your state offers state-run dispute resolution programs. If you suspect you have a vehicle problem that might fall under your state's lemon law, call your local or state consumer protection agency to find out about your rights under the lemon law.

If you have a safety problem with your vehicle, report it to the National Highway Traffic Safety Administration Auto Safety Hotline at 888-327-4236. NHTSA also provides recall and crash test information, but does not handle complaints. The administrator's website is located at **www.nhtsa.dot.gov.**

AUTOMOBILE CUSTOMER SERVICE DEPARTMENTS

ACURA
Customer Relations Department
1919 Torrance Blvd.
Torrance, CA 90501-2746
800-382-2238
www.acura.com

ALFA ROMEO DISTRIBUTORS OF NORTH AMERICA, INC.
7454 Brokerage
Orlando, FL 32809
407-856-5000
www.alfaromeo.com

AMERICAN HONDA MOTOR CO., INC.
Consumer Affairs Department
1919 Torrance Blvd.
Torrance, CA 90501-2746
310-783-2000
800-999-1009
www.honda.com

AMERICAN ISUZU MOTORS, INC.
Owner Relations Department
13340 183rd St.
Cerritos, CA 90702-6007
800-255-6727
www.isuzu.com

AMERICAN SUZUKI MOTOR CORP.
Customer Relations Department
PO Box 1100
3251 East Imperial Hwy
Brea, CA 92822-1100
714-996-7040, ext. 380 (motorcycles)
714-572-1490
800-934-0934 (automotive only)
www.suzuki.com

ASTON MARTIN, JAGUAR LANDROVER PREMIER AUTO GROUP
Customer Relations Department
U.S. National Headquarters
1 Premier Place
Irvine, CA 92618
949-341-6100
800-452-4827
www.jaguar.com

AUDI OF AMERICA, INC.
Client Relations
3499 West Hamlin Road
Rochester Hills, MI 48309
800-822-2834
www.audiusa.com

BMW OF NORTH AMERICA, INC.
300 Chestnut Ridge Rd.
Woodcliff Lake, NJ 07675
201-307-4000
800-831-1117
www.bmwusa.com

BUICK DIVISION GENERAL MOTORS CORP.
Customer Assistance Center
PO Box 33136
Detroit, MI 48232-5136
313-556-5000
800-521-7300
www.buick.com

CADILLAC MOTOR CAR DIVISION
Customer Assistance Center
PO Box 33169
Detroit, MI 48232-5169
800-458-8006
www.cadillac.com

CHEVROLET MOTOR DIVISION, GENERAL MOTORS CORP.
Customer Assistance Center
PO Box 33170
Detroit, MI 48232-5170
800-222-1020
www.chevrolet.com

DAIHATSU AMERICA, INC.
Consumer Affairs Department
28 Centerpointe Dr. Ste 120
La Palma, CA 90623
714-690-4700
800-777-7070
www.daihatsu.com/

DAIMLER CHRYSLER MOTORS CORP
See Chrysler, Plymouth, Dodge, Jeep
PO Box 21-8004
Auburn Hills, MI 48321-8004
800-992-1997
www.chrysler.com

FERRARI NORTH AMERICA INC.
250 Sylvan Ave.
Englewood Cliffs, NJ 07632
201-816-2600
www.ferrari.com

FORD MOTOR COMPANY
Customer Relationship Center
16800 Executive Plaza Dr.
P.O. Box 6248
Dearborn, MI 48121
800-392-3673
www.ford.com

GMC DIVISION GENERAL MOTORS CORP.
Customer Assistance Center
PO Box 33172
Detroit, MI 48232-5172
800-462-8782
www.gmc.com

HYUNDAI MOTOR AMERICA
Consumer Affairs
10550 Talbert Ave.
P.O. Box 20850
Fountain Valley, CA 92728-0850
714-965-3000
800-633-5151
www.hyundai.usa.com

KIA MOTORS AMERICA, INC.
Consumer Assistance Center
PO Box 52410
Irvine, CA 92619-2410
800-333-4KIA
www.kia.com

LEXUS
Toyota Motor Sales, U.S.A., Inc.
Customer Satisfaction Department
Mail Drop L203
19001 South Western Ave
Torrance, CA 90509-2732
800-25 LEXUS
www.lexus.com

MAZDA MOTOR OF AMERICA, INC.
Customer Relations Manager
Jamboree Plaza
4 Park Plaza, Suite 1250
Irvine, CA 92614
800-222-5500
www.mazdausa.com

MERCEDES BENZ OF NORTH AMERICA, INC.
Customer Assistance Center
3 Paragon Dr.
Montvale, NJ 07645
800-222-0100
www.mbusa.com

MITSUBISHI MOTOR SALES OF AMERICA, INC.
Customer Relations
6400 Katella Ave.
Cypress, CA 90630-0064
800-MITSU-2000
www.mitsubishimotors.com

NISSAN NORTH AMERICA, INC.
Consumer Affairs Group
PO Box 191
Gardena, CA 90248-0191
310-532-3111
800-647-7261
www.nissan-usa.com

OLDSMOBILE DIVISION GENERAL MOTORS CORP.
Customer Assistance Network
PO Box 33171
Detroit, MI 48232-5171
800-442-6537
www.oldsmobile.com

PEUGEOT MOTORS OF AMERICA, INC.
Consumer Relations
Overlook at Great Notch
150 Clove Road
Little Falls, NJ 07424
973-812-4444
800-345-5545
www.peugeot.com

PONTIAC DIVISION, GENERAL MOTORS CORP.
Customer Assistance Center
P.O. Box 33172
Detroit, MI 48232-5172
800-762-2737
www.gm.com

PORSCHE CARS NORTH AMERICA, INC.
Owner Relations
980 Hammond Dr. Suite 1000
Atlanta, GA 30328
770-290-3500
800-545-8039
www.porsche.com

SAAB CARS USA, INC.
Customer Assistance Center
4405-A International Blvd
Norcross, GA 30093
770-279-0100
800-955-9007
www.saabusa.com

SATURN CORPORATION, DIVISION OF GENERAL MOTORS CORP.
Saturn Customer Assistance Center
100 Saturn Parkway
Spring Hill, TN 37174
931-486-5050
800-553-6000
www.saturn.com

SUBARU OF AMERICA, INC.
National Customer Service Center
Subaru Plaza, PO Box 6000
Cherry Hill, NJ 08002
856-488-8500
800-782-2783
www.subaru.com

TOYOTA MOTOR SALES USA, INC.
Customer Assistance Center
Department H200
19001 S. Western Avenue
Torrance, CA 90509
310-468-4000
800-331-4331
www.toyota.com

VOLKSWAGEN OF AMERICA
Customer Relations
Hills Corporate Center
3499 West Hamlin Rd.
Rochester Hills, MI 48309
800-DRIVE VW
800-822-8987
www.vw.com

VOLVO CARS OF NORTH AMERICA
Customer Service
PO Box 914
7 Volvo Drive, Building A
Rockleigh, NJ 07647-0915
800-458-1552
www.volvocars.com

ALTERNATIVE DISPUTE RESOLUTION PROGRAMS

Center for Auto Safety (CAS)
1825 Connecticut Ave., NW Suite 330
Washington, DC 20009
202-328-7700, ext. 107
www.autosafety.org

CAS advocates on behalf of consumers in auto safety and quality, fuel efficiency, emissions, and related issues. For advice on specific problems, CAS requests that consumers write a brief statement of the problem or question, include: the year, make, model of the vehicle, and a stamped self-addressed envelope.

Council of Better Business Bureaus, Inc.
4200 Wilson Blvd., Suite 800
Arlington, VA 22203-1838
703-276-0100
800-955-5100
Fax: 703-525-8277
www.bbb.org

Office of Defects Investigation

DOT Auto Safety Hotline
400 7th Street SW
Washington, DC 20590
888-DASH-2-DOT
800-424-9153
www.nhtsa.dot.gov/hotline

Consumers can contact the DOT Auto Safety Hotline to report safety defects in vehicles, tires, and child safety seats. Information is available about air bags, child safety seats, seat belts, and general highway safety. Consumers who experience a safety defect in their vehicle are encouraged to report the defect to the Hotline in addition to the dealer or manufacturer.

International Association of Lemon Law Administrators

www.TheLemonLaw.org

This organization supports and promotes government agencies that administer motor vehicle warranty and related laws, through the publication of a newsletter, consumer and industry education, and other intergovernmental activities.

Motorist Assurance Program

7101 Wisconsin Ave
Suite 1200
Bethesda, MD 20814
301-634-4954
301-634-4955
www.motorist.org

MAP accredits auto repair shops that apply and follow industry developed standards for inspecting vehicles. It also meets other requirements, handles inquiries/disputes between accredited shops and customers, and offers information to consumers about how to locate a repair shop; how to talk to a technician; and, how to gain satisfaction from auto repair shops.

National Automobile Dealers Association

8400 Westpark Dr.
McLean, VA 22102
703-821-7000
800-252-6232
www.nada.org

Third-party dispute resolution program administered through the National Automobile Dealers Association. Consumer information available on request.

National Institute for Automotive Service Excellence (ASE)

101 Blue Seal Dr. SE, Suite 101
Leesburg, VA 20175
703-669-6600
www.asecert.org

ASE is an independent, national, nonprofit organization founded in 1972 to help improve the quality of automotive service and repair through the voluntary testing and certification of automotive repair professionals. ASE publishes several consumer publications about auto maintenance and repair.

RV Consumer Group

PO Box 520
Quilcene, WA 98376
800-405-3325
www.rv.org

Nonprofit organization dedicated to the safety of recreational vehicles.

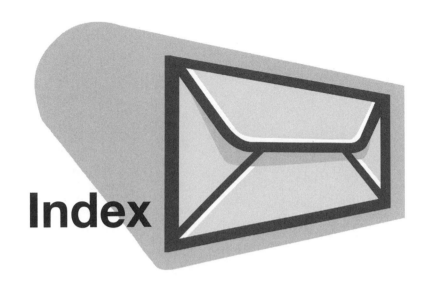

Index

A

accidents, 5
administrative costs, 1
advertising fees, 1
age discrimination, 37, 46
Age Discrimination in Employment Act., 37, 46
AIDS, 112
airlines, 155, 156, 157, 160, 163, 164, 169
American Society of Travel Agents, 157, 167
Americans with Disabilities Act (ADA), 36, 44, 45, 156, 157, 164
Amtrak, 158
annual percentage rate (APR), 5
Anti-Defamation League, 35
Association for Advancement of Retired People (AARP), 35
automobiles. *See cars*

B

bankruptcy, 60, 157
banks, 56, 62, 68, 69, 70, 112, 127, 128, 129
Better Business Bureau, 4, 6, 7, 22, 110, 111, 157
billing errors, 85, 96, 99
bullying, 142, 143, 149, 150, 152
bumped passengers, 157, 169

C

cable television, 111, 121
car rentals, 159, 179
cars, 1–6
child pornography, 19
children, 141, 142, 144

Civil Rights Act of 1964, 35
    Title VII, 37
claims, 5
class action suits, 4, 5, 6
collection agencies, 56, 57, 71, 72, 90, 107, 110
compensation, 35
computers, 17, 21, 23, 24, 53, 115
consumer credit, 5
consumer protection, 4
contractors, 110
credit card companies, 53, 54, 62–67, 81, 110
credit cards, 54, 55, 58, 60, 115
Credit Life Insurance, 6, 15
credit reporting agencies, 58, 73, 74
credit reports, 57, 58, 73, 74
creditors, 56
customer service, 21
cyberspace, 19, 53

D

damaged luggage, 155, 161
damaged merchandise, 55, 63
dealers, 1–7
debit cards, 19, 55, 58, 68, 69, 70
debt collectors, 110
debts, 56, 71, 72, 90, 107
defective repairs, 1
delay notices, 115
denial of coverage, 86
Department of Health and Human Services, 84, 91, 95
Department of Homeland Security, 155
Department of Housing and Urban Development, 112

Department of Justice, 112
Department of Transportation, 2, 156, 157, 161, 163, 164, 165
diabetics, 156
digital subscriber line (DSL), 18
disabilities, 36, 44, 45, 112, 141, 144, 156, 158, 164, 173
discrimination, 35, 37, 40, 41, 112, 123, 125
disputed charges, 64
divorce, 55, 60, 67
Do Not Call Registry, 109, 114, 130, 131, 132

E

education, 141, 146
emails, 20, 115, 135, 136
employee records, 38, 50, 51
employment, 35
Equal Employment Opportunity Commission (EEOC), 35, 36, 37, 39
Equal Pay Act, 36, 43
evictions, 60

F

Fair Credit Billing Act, 115
Fair Debt Collection Practices Act, 56, 90
Fair Housing Act, 112
familial status, 112, 125
Family and Medical Leave Act (FMLA), 37, 48, 49
Federal Aviation Administration, 155
Federal Trade Commission, 19, 20, 21, 57, 58, 62, 113, 114, 115, 136, 139
finance, 4, 5, 53
firing, 35
foreclosure, 60
Freddie Mac, 113
Freddie Mae, 113

G

gender, 35, 112
guarantees, 2

H

hackers, 18, 19
hardware, 17
health, 83, 100
Health Insurance Portability and Accountability Act of 1996 (HIPAA), 84
healthcare power of attorney, 89, 105
Hill-Burton Act, 87, 101
hiring, 35
HIV, 112
home, 109, 117, 126

improvements, 110, 119
Homeowner's Protection Act, 113
hospital accreditation, 87
hospitals, 58, 76
hotels, 157, 171, 173, 175
housing discrimination, 112

I

identity theft, 19, 28, 53, 58, 62
Identity Theft and Assumption Deterrence Act of 1998, 58
Individualized Education Plan (IEP), 141, 142, 143, 146
Individualized Educational Evaluation (IEE), 142, 147
Individuals with Educational Disabilities Act (IDEA), 141
insurance, 5, 13, 14
insurance companies, 58, 75, 76, 83, 85, 86, 90, 96–99, 100
interest rates, 60, 81, 110, 115, 140
Internet crimes, 19, 26, 28
Internet service providers, 18, 20, 26, 31, 32
Internet service providers , 115, 133, 134

J

Joint Commission on Accreditation of Healthcare Organizations, 88

L

landlords, 109, 110, 112, 117
late fees, 66
learning disabilities, 144
lemon laws, 1, 2, 7, 8
living wills, 89, 104, 105
loan processing, 1
lost credit cards, 55
luggage, 155, 156, 160, 161, 163

M

manufacturers, 2, 3, 7, 12
mechanics, 2, 3
Medicaid, 87
Medicare, 83
mileage, 3
military, 60, 81, 110, 115, 140
mortgage payments, 60
mutual funds, 59

N

National Association for Advancement of Colored People (NAACP), 35

National Highway Traffic Safety Administration, 2
National Organization for Women (NOW), 35
national origin, 35, 112
nursing homes, 88, 91, 103

O

odometers, 2, 3, 7, 10, 11, 12
Office of Civil Rights, 84, 158
Office of the Comptroller of the Currency, 56
ombudsman, 88
online bill paying, 54
online purchases, 19, 22, 29, 30
orders , 137, 138

P

paperwork fees, 1
patches, 17
paternity leave, 48
patients, 87, 101, 104, 105
payment processing, 55
personal identification numbers, 55
personnel files, 38, 50, 51
power of attorney, 89, 104, 105
prescriptions, 85, 90, 97, 98, 106, 156, 165
printers, 17
privacy officer, 84
Private Mortgage Insurance (PMI), 109, 113, 127, 128, 129
processing fees, 1
provider relations departments, 58

R

race, 35, 40, 112, 123
rebuilt parts, 5, 13
religion, 35, 41, 112
repairs, 2, 13
rescission, 3
right to privacy, 83, 92, 94, 95
Rule 240, 157

S

sales contracts, 1
scanners, 17
schools, 141, 142, 143, 147, 149, 150, 152
Section 8, 109, 112
securities, 59, 77, 78
Securities and Exchange Commission (SEC), 18, 59, 78, 79
security deposits, 109, 112, 126
sexual harassment, 35, 37, 47
SF95, 156
Small Claims Court, 111, 157

Social Security Administration, 62
software, 17, 18, 22, 25
Soldier's and Sailor's Relief Act of 1940, 60, 115, 140
spam, 20, 31, 32, 115, 133
special education, 142
stalking, 19
statements, 65
stocks, 59
stolen credit cards, 55
substandard insurance companies, 5
suggestive pictures, 37
syringes, 156, 165

T

taxicabs, 158, 178
telemarketers, 114
Telephone Consumer Protection Act, 114
tenants, 109, 110, 112, 117
threatening, 37
trains, 158, 177
Transportation Security Agency, 156, 161, 163, 165
travel, 155
    agents, 157, 158, 167

U

unauthorized use, 54, 55, 67, 68, 69, 70
unequal pay, 43
uninsured, 87, 101
utilities, 111, 122

V

vehicle identification number, 3
vehicles. *See cars*

W

warehousing fees, 1
warranties, 2, 7, 17
warranty work, 2
wheelchairs, 158, 164, 173

Z

zone offices, 7

About the Author

Janet Rubel is an Illinois attorney. She is a graduate of Washington University in St. Louis and Illinois Institute of Technology Chicago-Kent School of Law. The author has practiced law for more years than she cares to admit.

Ms. Rubel has been an adjunct faculty member at Harper College teaching probate law for paralegals and John Marshall Law School teaching advanced appellate practice. Her law school students fared well in the school's moot court competitions.

The author has won some notable cases in the Illinois Appellate Court that have attracted national attention. Ms. Rubel convinced the Illinois Appellate Court to rule that attorneys preying sexually on their vulnerable clients is unethical in *Marriage of Kantar*. She took the seemingly hopeless case of a woman whose divorce attorney initiated a sexual relationship with her during the divorce. This was the first time the Illinois appellate court addressed this type of problem.

Another Illinois case of note won by the author is a post-divorce case limiting the college education expenses a divorced parent is required to pay, *Greiman v. Friedman*. She represented a father who was ordered to pay college expenses for a daughter who was not a diligent student and for another daughter who was a good student at a very expensive private university. Ms. Rubel persuaded the Illinois Appellate Court to limit the father's financial obligations.

Visit her website at:
www.101complaints.org

Your #1 Source for Real World Legal Information...

SPHINX® PUBLISHING
An Imprint of Sourcebooks, Inc.®

• Written by lawyers
• Simple English explanation of the law
• Forms and instructions included

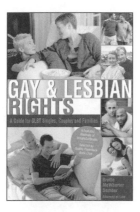

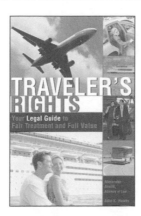

Gay & Lesbian Rights

This comprehensive guide explains the limited legal protection available for the GLBT community. It includes extensive appendices that provide state-specific references including Vermont's Civil Union Statute and California's Domestic Partnership Law.

296 pages; $26.95;
ISBN 1-57248-331-8

Traveler's Rights

Use this guide as a home reference or take it with you on your journeys. From booking your trip through a travel agent to what extra hotel charges are actually legit, this book is a must have for every traveler.

304 pages; $21.95;
ISBN 1-57248-335-0

Teen Rights

This book discusses topics ranging from dress codes to curfews, as well as more serious topics like discrimination, drug abuse, and pregnancy. State-by-state references of specific laws are included.

344 pages; $22.95;
ISBN 1-57248-221-4

See the following order form for books written specifically for California,
the District of Columbia, Florida, Georgia, Illinois, Maryland, Massachusetts, Michigan,
Minnesota, New Jersey, New York, North Carolina,
Ohio, Pennsylvania, Texas, and Virginia!

What our customers say about our books:

"It couldn't be more clear for the lay person." —R.D.

"I want you to know I really appreciate your book. It has saved me a lot of time and money." —L.T.

"Your real estate contracts book has saved me nearly $12,000.00 in closing costs over the past year." —A.B.

"...many of the legal questions that I have had over the years were answered clearly and concisely through your plain English interpretation of the law." —C.E.H.

"If there weren't people out there like you I'd be lost. You have the best books of this type out there." —S.B.

"...your forms and directions are easy to follow." —C.V.M.

Sphinx Publishing's Legal Survival Guides
are directly available from Sourcebooks, Inc., or from your local bookstores.

For credit card orders call 1–800–432–7444, write P.O. Box 4410, Naperville, IL 60567-4410,
or fax 630-961-2168

Find more legal information at: **www.SphinxLegal.com**

Sphinx® Publishing's National Titles
Valid in All 50 States

Legal Survival in Business

The Complete Book of Corporate Forms	$24.95
The Complete Patent Book	$26.95
The Entrepreneur's Internet Handbook	$21.95
How to Form a Limited Liability Company (2E)	$24.95
Incorporate in Delaware from Any State	$24.95
Incorporate in Nevada from Any State	$24.95
How to Form a Nonprofit Corporation (2E)	$24.95
How to Form Your Own Corporation (4E)	$26.95
How to Form Your Own Partnership (2E)	$24.95
How to Register Your Own Copyright (4E)	$24.95
How to Register Your Own Trademark (3E)	$21.95
Most Valuable Business Legal Forms You'll Ever Need (3E)	$21.95
Profit from Intellectual Property	$28.95
Protect Your Patent	$24.95
The Small Business Owner's Guide to Bankruptcy	$21.95

Legal Survival in Court

Attorney Responsibilities & Client Rights	$19.95
Crime Victim's Guide to Justice (2E)	$21.95
Grandparents' Rights (3E)	$24.95
Help Your Lawyer Win Your Case (2E)	$14.95
Jurors' Rights (2E)	$12.95
Legal Research Made Easy (3E)	$21.95
Winning Your Personal Injury Claim (2E)	$24.95
Your Rights When You Owe Too Much	$16.95

Legal Survival in Real Estate

Essential Guide to Real Estate Contracts (2E)	$18.95
Essential Guide to Real Estate Leases	$18.95
How to Buy a Condominium or Townhome (2E)	$19.95
How to Buy Your First Home	$18.95
Working with Your Homeowners Association	$19.95

Legal Survival in Personal Affairs

The 529 College Savings Plan	$16.95
The Antique and Art Collector's Legal Guide	$24.95
Cómo Hacer su Propio Testamento	$16.95
Cómo Restablecer su propio Crédito y Renegociar sus Deudas	$21.95
Cómo Solicitar su Propio Divorcio	$24.95
The Complete Legal Guide to Senior Care	$21.95
Credit Smart	$18.95
Family Limited Partnership	$26.95
Gay & Lesbian Rights	$26.95
Guía de Inmigración a Estados Unidos (3E)	$24.95
Guía de Justicia para Víctimas del Crimen	$21.95
How to File Your Own Bankruptcy (5E)	$21.95
How to File Your Own Divorce (5E)	$26.95
How to Make Your Own Simple Will (3E)	$18.95
How to Write Your Own Living Will (3E)	$18.95
How to Write Your Own Premarital Agreement (3E)	$24.95
Inmigración a los EE. UU. Paso a Paso	$22.95
Living Trusts and Other Ways to Avoid Probate (3E)	$24.95
Manual de Beneficios para el Seguro Social	$18.95
Mastering the MBE	$16.95
Most Valuable Personal Legal Forms You'll Ever Need (2E)	$26.95
Neighbor v. Neighbor (2E)	$16.95
The Nanny and Domestic Help Legal Kit	$22.95
The Power of Attorney Handbook (4E)	$19.95
Repair Your Own Credit and Deal with Debt (2E)	$18.95
El Seguro Social Preguntas y Respuestas	$14.95
Sexual Harassment:Your Guide to Legal Action	$18.95
The Social Security Benefits Handbook (3E)	$18.95
Social Security Q&A	$12.95
Teen Rights	$22.95
Traveler's Rights	$21.95
Unmarried Parents' Rights (2E)	$19.95
U.S. Immigration and Citizenship Q&A	$16.95
U.S. Immigration Step by Step	$21.95
U.S.A. Immigration Guide (4E)	$24.95
The Visitation Handbook	$18.95
The Wills, Estate Planning and Trusts Legal Kit	$26.95
Win Your Unemployment Compensation Claim (2E)	$21.95
Your Right to Child Custody, Visitation and Support (2E)	$24.95

SPHINX® PUBLISHING ORDER FORM

BILL TO:			SHIP TO:		
Phone #		Terms	F.O.B.	Chicago, IL	Ship Date

Charge my: ☐ VISA   ☐ MasterCard   ☐ American Express

☐ **Money Order or Personal Check**

Credit Card Number   Expiration Date

Qty	ISBN	Title	Retail	Ext.	Qty	ISBN	Title	Retail	Ext.
		SPHINX PUBLISHING NATIONAL TITLES				1-57248-169-2	The Power of Attorney Handbook (4E)	$19.95	
	1-57248-238-9	The 529 College Savings Plan	$16.95			1-57248-332-6	Profit from Intellectual Property	$28.95	
	1-57248-349-0	The Antique and Art Collector's Legal Guide	$24.95			1-57248-329-6	Protect Your Patent	$24.95	
	1-57248-347-4	Attorney Responsibilities & Client Rights	$19.95			1-57248-344-X	Repair Your Own Credit and Deal with Debt (2E)	$18.95	
	1-57248-148-X	Cómo Hacer su Propio Testamento	$16.95			1-57248-350-4	El Seguro Social Preguntas y Respuestas	$14.95	
	1-57248-226-5	Cómo Restablecer su propio Crédito y Renegociar sus Deudas	$21.95			1-57248-217-6	Sexual Harassment: Your Guide to Legal Action	$18.95	
	1-57248-147-1	Cómo Solicitar su Propio Divorcio	$24.95			1-57248-219-2	The Small Business Owner's Guide to Bankruptcy	$21.95	
	1-57248-166-8	The Complete Book of Corporate Forms	$24.95			1-57248-168-4	The Social Security Benefits Handbook (3E)	$18.95	
	1-57248-229-X	The Complete Legal Guide to Senior Care	$21.95			1-57248-216-8	Social Security Q&A	$12.95	
	1-57248-201-X	The Complete Patent Book	$26.95			1-57248-221-4	Teen Rights	$22.95	
	1-57248-163-3	Crime Victim's Guide to Justice (2E)	$21.95			1-57248-335-0	Traveler's Rights	$21.95	
	1-57248-251-6	The Entrepreneur's Internet Handbook	$21.95			1-57248-236-2	Unmarried Parents' Rights (2E)	$19.95	
	1-57248-346-6	Essential Guide to Real Estate Contracts (2E)	$18.95			1-57248-218-4	U.S. Immigration Step by Step	$21.95	
	1-57248-160-9	Essential Guide to Real Estate Leases	$18.95			1-57248-161-7	U.S.A. Immigration Guide (4E)	$24.95	
	1-57248-254-0	Family Limited Partnership	$26.95			1-57248-192-7	The Visitation Handbook	$18.95	
	1-57248-331-8	Gay & Lesbian Rights	$26.95			1-57248-225-7	Win Your Unemployment Compensation Claim (2E)	$21.95	
	1-57248-139-0	Grandparents' Rights (3E)	$24.95			1-57248-330-X	The Wills, Estate Planning and Trusts Legal Kit	&26.95	
	1-57248-188-9	Guía de Inmigración a Estados Unidos (3E)	$24.95			1-57248-138-2	Winning Your Personal Injury Claim (2E)	$24.95	
	1-57248-187-0	Guía de Justicia para Víctimas del Crimen	$21.95			1-57248-333-4	Working with Your Homeowners Association	$19.95	
	1-57248-103-X	Help Your Lawyer Win Your Case (2E)	$14.95			1-57248-162-5	Your Right to Child Custody, Visitation and Support (2E)	$24.95	
	1-57248-164-1	How to Buy a Condominium or Townhome (2E)	$19.95			1-57248-157-9	Your Rights When You Owe Too Much	$16.95	
	1-57248-328-8	How to Buy Your First Home	$18.95				**CALIFORNIA TITLES**		
	1-57248-191-9	How to File Your Own Bankruptcy (5E)	$21.95			1-57248-150-1	CA Power of Attorney Handbook (2E)	$18.95	
	1-57248-343-1	How to File Your Own Divorce (5E)	$26.95			1-57248-337-7	How to File for Divorce in CA (4E)	$26.95	
	1-57248-222-2	How to Form a Limited Liability Company (2E)	$24.95			1-57248-145-5	How to Probate and Settle an Estate in CA	$26.95	
	1-57248-231-1	How to Form a Nonprofit Corporation (2E)	$24.95			1-57248-336-9	How to Start a Business in CA (2E)	$21.95	
	1-57248-345-8	How to Form Your Own Corporation (4E)	$26.95			1-57248-194-3	How to Win in Small Claims Court in CA (2E)	$18.95	
	1-57248-224-9	How to Form Your Own Partnership (2E)	$24.95			1-57248-246-X	Make Your Own CA Will	$18.95	
	1-57248-232-X	How to Make Your Own Simple Will (3E)	$18.95			1-57248-196-X	The Landlord's Legal Guide in CA	$24.95	
	1-57248-200-1	How to Register Your Own Copyright (4E)	$24.95			1-57248-241-9	Tenants' Rights in CA	$21.95	
	1-57248-104-8	How to Register Your Own Trademark (3E)	$21.95				**FLORIDA TITLES**		
	1-57248-233-8	How to Write Your Own Living Will (3E)	$18.95			1-57071-363-4	Florida Power of Attorney Handbook (2E)	$16.95	
	1-57248-156-0	How to Write Your Own Premarital Agreement (3E)	$24.95			1-57248-176-5	How to File for Divorce in FL (7E)	$26.95	
	1-57248-230-3	Incorporate in Delaware from Any State	$24.95			1-57248-356-0	How to Form a Corporation in FL (6E)	$24.95	
	1-57248-158-7	Incorporate in Nevada from Any State	$24.95			1-57248-203-6	How to Form a Limited Liability Co. in FL (2E)	$24.95	
	1-57248-250-8	Inmigración a los EE.UU. Paso a Paso	$22.95			1-57071-401-0	How to Form a Partnership in FL	$22.95	
	1-57071-333-2	Jurors' Rights (2E)	$12.95			1-57248-113-7	How to Make a FL Will (6E)	$16.95	
	1-57248-223-0	Legal Research Made Easy (3E)	$21.95			1-57248-088-2	How to Modify Your FL Divorce Judgment (4E)	$24.95	
	1-57248-165-X	Living Trusts and Other Ways to Avoid Probate (3E)	$24.95			1-57248-144-7	How to Probate and Settle an Estate in FL (4E)	$26.95	
	1-57248-186-2	Manual de Beneficios para el Seguro Social	$18.95			1-57248-339-3	How to Start a Business in FL (7E)	$21.95	
	1-57248-220-6	Mastering the MBE	$16.95			1-57248-204-4	How to Win in Small Claims Court in FL (7E)	$18.95	
	1-57248-167-6	Most Val. Business Legal Forms You'll Ever Need (3E)	$21.95			1-57248-202-8	Land Trusts in Florida (6E)	$29.95	
	1-57248-360-1	Most Val. Personal Legal Forms You'll Ever Need (2E)	$26.95			1-57248-338-5	Landlords' Rights and Duties in FL (9E)	$22.95	
	1-57248-098-X	The Nanny and Domestic Help Legal Kit	$22.95			***Form Continued on Following Page***		**SUBTOTAL**	
	1-57248-089-0	Neighbor v. Neighbor (2E)	$16.95						

To order, call Sourcebooks at 1-800-432-7444 or FAX (630) 961-2168 (Bookstores, libraries, wholesalers—please call for discount)

Prices are subject to change without notice.

Find more legal information at: **www.SphinxLegal.com**

SPHINX® PUBLISHING ORDER FORM

Qty	ISBN	Title	Retail	Ext.
		GEORGIA TITLES		
___	1-57248-340-7	How to File for Divorce in GA (5E)	$21.95	___
___	1-57248-180-3	How to Make a GA Will (4E)	$21.95	___
___	1-57248-341-5	How to Start a Business in Georgia (3E)	$21.95	___
		ILLINOIS TITLES		
___	1-57248-244-3	Child Custody, Visitation, and Support in IL	$24.95	___
___	1-57248-206-0	How to File for Divorce in IL (3E)	$24.95	___
___	1-57248-170-6	How to Make an IL Will (3E)	$16.95	___
___	1-57248-247-8	How to Start a Business in IL (3E)	$21.95	___
___	1-57248-252-4	The Landlord's Legal Guide in IL	$24.95	___
		MARYLAND, VIRGINIA AND THE DISTRICT OF COLUMBIA		
___	1-57248-240-0	How to File for Divorce in MD, VA and DC	$28.95	___
___	1-57248-359-8	How to Start a Business in MD, VA or DC	$21.95	___
		MASSACHUSETTS TITLES		
___	1-57248-128-5	How to File for Divorce in MA (3E)	$24.95	___
___	1-57248-115-3	How to Form a Corporation in MA	$24.95	___
___	1-57248-108-0	How to Make a MA Will (2E)	$16.95	___
___	1-57248-248-6	How to Start a Business in MA (3E)	$21.95	___
___	1-57248-209-5	The Landlord's Legal Guide in MA	$24.95	___
		MICHIGAN TITLES		
___	1-57248-215-X	How to File for Divorce in MI (3E)	$24.95	___
___	1-57248-182-X	How to Make a MI Will (3E)	$16.95	___
___	1-57248-183-8	How to Start a Business in MI (3E)	$18.95	___
		MINNESOTA TITLES		
___	1-57248-142-0	How to File for Divorce in MN	$21.95	___
___	1-57248-179-X	How to Form a Corporation in MN	$24.95	___
___	1-57248-178-1	How to Make a MN Will (2E)	$16.95	___
		NEW JERSEY TITLES		
___	1-57248-239-7	How to File for Divorce in NJ	$24.95	___
		NEW YORK TITLES		
___	1-57248-193-5	Child Custody, Visitation and Support in NY	$26.95	___
___	1-57248-351-2	File for Divorce in NY	$26.95	___
___	1-57248-249-4	How to Form a Corporation in NY (2E)	$24.95	___
___	1-57248-095-5	How to Make a NY Will (2E)	$16.95	___
___	1-57248-199-4	How to Start a Business in NY (2E)	$18.95	___
___	1-57248-198-6	How to Win in Small Claims Court in NY (2E)	$18.95	___
___	1-57248-197-8	Landlords' Legal Guide in NY	$24.95	___
___	1-57071-188-7	New York Power of Attorney Handbook	$19.95	___
___	1-57248-122-6	Tenants' Rights in NY	$21.95	___

Qty	ISBN	Title	Retail	Ext.
		NORTH CAROLINA TITLES		
___	1-57248-185-4	How to File for Divorce in NC (3E)	$22.95	___
___	1-57248-129-3	How to Make a NC Will (3E)	$16.95	___
___	1-57248-184-6	How to Start a Business in NC (3E)	$18.95	___
___	1-57248-091-2	Landlords' Rights & Duties in NC	$21.95	___
		OHIO TITLES		
___	1-57248-190-0	How to File for Divorce in OH (2E)	$24.95	___
___	1-57248-174-9	How to Form a Corporation in OH	$24.95	___
___	1-57248-173-0	How to Make an OH Will	$16.95	___
		PENNSYLVANIA TITLES		
___	1-57248-242-7	Child Custody, Visitation and Support in PA	$26.95	___
___	1-57248-211-7	How to File for Divorce in PA (3E)	$26.95	___
___	1-57248-358-X	How to Form a Corporation in PA	$24.95	___
___	1-57248-094-7	How to Make a PA Will (2E)	$16.95	___
___	1-57248-357-1	How to Start a Business in PA (3E)	$21.95	___
___	1-57248-245-1	The Landlord's Legal Guide in PA	$24.95	___
		TEXAS TITLES		
___	1-57248-171-4	Child Custody, Visitation, and Support in TX	$22.95	___
___	1-57248-172-2	How to File for Divorce in TX (3E)	$24.95	___
___	1-57248-114-5	How to Form a Corporation in TX (2E)	$24.95	___
___	1-57248-255-9	How to Make a TX Will (3E)	$16.95	___
___	1-57248-214-1	How to Probate and Settle an Estate in TX (3E)	$26.95	___
___	1-57248-228-1	How to Start a Business in TX (3E)	$18.95	___
___	1-57248-111-0	How to Win in Small Claims Court in TX (2E)	$16.95	___
___	1-57248-355-5	the Landlord's Legal Guide in TX	$24.95	___

SUBTOTAL THIS PAGE ___

SUBTOTAL PREVIOUS PAGE ___

Shipping — $5.00 for 1st book, $1.00 each additional ___

Illinois residents add 6.75% sales tax ___

Connecticut residents add 6.00% sales tax ___

TOTAL ___

To order, call Sourcebooks at 1-800-432-7444 or FAX (630) 961-2168 (Bookstores, libraries, wholesalers—please call for discount)
Prices are subject to change without notice.
Find more legal information at: **www.SphinxLegal.com**